THIS BOOK IS FOR YOU IF...

- You suffer from daily stress and want a more peaceful and relaxed life
- You need a strategy to manage your interactions with those around you
- You have a team that needs to develop some coping strategies
- You need a process to make personal changes work
- You want to enjoy your life and feel better

We only have one life; make it happy with less stress and enjoy it more.

WHAT PEOPLE ARE SAYING

I found the Caveman Principals to be a witty, humerous and easy to follow self help guide based on the premis that stress and your reactions to it are the main cause of angst, anxiety, worry and self deprecating beliefs.

Using and sharing his own experiences, Carl Jones has managed to unpack, using simple, clear language the common threads of DISC and MBTI to condense these into a Caveperson analogy that struck a cord with me and I've used this insight to shape my thinking around inter personal communication in the workplace and what motivates me to enjoy my life.

As a 'Hunter' with a fair degree of 'Protector' thrown in, I've re-assessed my family and close associates into the Cavepeople and this has opened up better communication between the people I love and the various teams I lead, which of course leads to better results and happier people.

Personally, continuing the Caveman analogy of internal change management utilising the 'Herder' and the 'Mammoth' not only led to some genuine laugh out loud moments, but quiet reflection on the times I'd let my Herder try to short cut the journey and derail the Mammoth!

I've read a number of business related psychological based books, to further my work and mitigate stress 'triggers' and feel that The Caveman Principals should be right up there as a soft introduction to this area.

Mark Pearce, CEO & Director – JPR Environmental, Instant Insight Business Accounting and ANLIE.

I have just returned from a prehistoric adventure with "The Caveman Principles" by Carl Jones! This delightful self-help book is like having a quirky caveman buddy guiding you through the modern jungle of stress and communication.

Carl tackles the age-old struggle of stress management, revealing that our anxiety can be traced back to our ancestors' trusty (and sometimes overly excited) fight-or-flight responses. Who knew that dealing with deadlines and social media pressures could be so... primal?

Enter the "Caveman Tribe Sorter"—a clever and witty system that categorizes folks into four unique tribes based on how they communicate. Knowing your tribe can be as enlightening as discovering you have a long-lost dinosaur relative. It's a game changer for improving relationships!

Not only is the book packed with practical tips, but it's written with such humor and accessibility that you'll find yourself chuckling while learning to herd your metaphorical pet Mammoth (my particular favourite) through the chaos of life. I mean, who wouldn't want to tame a Mammoth while navigating change?

So, if you're eager to understand your stress responses, enhance your relationships, and take charge of your well-being, grab a copy of "The Caveman Principles"! It's a fun, empowering read that proves you can manage stress without shouting "CAVE!" at every challenge. Plus, you might just discover your inner caveman (or cavewoman) along the way!

Bob Strange
THE CLOSER SPEAKERS CONSULTANCY LTD
https://thecloser.consulting/

Caveman Principles provides practical and valuable insights into understanding and managing stress. The book is both informative and entertaining and written in an accessible style. Caveman Principles is highly recommended to anyone looking to increase their understanding of stress in themselves and others and strategies to manage both effectively.

Jane French
www.therightaddress.co.uk

WHERE DID ALL THIS STRESS COME FROM?

Many, many years ago, it started with our Caveman ancestors. They developed a simple but effective survival technique designed to keep them alive. I call it the 'button' (Doctors will call it the adrenal medulla gland), which they could push whenever needed.

This button is just a tiny gland that sits on top of their kidneys. When threatened and they needed something extra, a press of this button produced adrenaline, and it discharged straight into the bloodstream. It primed their muscles to either stand their ground and fight or run away into flight mode. This fight or flight button helped them in many ways, from making them more reactive, stronger and more robust, allowing clearer thinking, and giving them superhuman strength when needed. If our Caveman ancestors came face to face with a Mammoth, pushing their button gave them what they needed.

Forty thousand years later, homo-sapiens (which in Latin terms means wise humans) still have that life-saving button. However, as there are no Mammoths around, do we still need it?

The truth may surprise you: Mammoths are still here!

If you could persuade today's Mammoths to enter and compete, they would win the National Hide and Seek Championship. Mammoths are sneaky and underhanded. They have mastered the art of hiding in plain sight in everyday situations, such as camouflaging in traffic jams and hiding behind passive-aggressive emails.

Anywhere that stress can thrive, you will find a hairy mammoth ready to pounce. They show themselves for a fraction of a second and only to their intended victim, just long enough to make you push your button!

The Caveman Principles help you control this reaction, easing interactions with others while reducing stress. They are suitable for individuals and teams.

ABOUT THE AUTHOR

Carl Jones is a motivational speaker, coach and trainer. Having worked in a particularly stressful environment as a front-line police officer, he observed first-hand the harmful effects of stress on people, including himself. Reducing stress became his mission, described as an obsession by those closest to him! His research into the subject helped him create The Caveman Principles, The S.L.A.P. Technique, The Capacity/Need/Want framework and his motivational speaking business.

Carl delivers engaging talks and shares real-life stories, lessons, and theories to help those suffering from stress. He leaves audiences with a new understanding of stress and feeling better about everyday life. His mission is to work with people who need his help, teaching the Caveman Principles to conquer stress.

Writing and publishing this book has given him a greater reach, a platform to help more people cope with everyday stress.

DEDICATION

To my incredible wife, Laura, thank you for putting up with me and for your input and support while I was writing this in my caveman world.

To all those who have bravely worn or continue to wear a uniform, selflessly serving communities and our Country, this book is also dedicated to the cause. Your resilience and dedication are massively under-appreciated.

The simple solution to burnout and stress

THE CAVEMAN PRINCIPLES

Stress is not set in stone
CARL JONES
"From Stress to success in easy steps"

Published in the United Kingdom by
Filament Publishing Ltd

14 Croydon Road,
Waddon, Croydon
Surrey, CR0 4PA

www.filamentpublishing.com
+44(0)20 8688 2598

The Caveman Principles by Carl Jones
ISBN 978-1-915465-81-8
© 2025 Carl Jones

Carl Jones asserts the right to be identified as the author of this work in accordance with the Designs and Copyright Act 1988

All rights reserved. No portion of this book may be copied in any way without the prior written permission of the publishers.

Printed in the UK

The Cavemen Principles Tribe images, depicting the Cavemen and Mammoths, are an integral part of this publication and as such are covered by this copyright. Note: While the information, advice and opinions expressed in this book are given in good faith, no liability can be accepted for loss or expense incurred as a result of relying on any statement made herein.

TABLE OF CONTENTS

	Where do we start?	13
	Using this book	15

Part 1

1.	The Origins of Stress	19
2.	Fight, Flight or Freeze	29
3.	Look out for stress Mammoths	39
4.	Don't Push the Button	67

Part 2

5.	People Profiling	105
6.	Using the CTS for the People in 'Our Tribe'	116
7.	Hunters	125
8.	Protectors	149
9.	Gatherers	171
10.	Healers	205
11.	Get a Tribe that works	227

Part 3

12.	Making a Change	242
13.	The Caveman Herder and the pet Mammoth	261
14.	Plan the Route	285
15.	Picture it	307
16.	Managing Resistance	325
17.	Celebrate the Milestones	334
18.	Reach the Destination	349
19.	Bonus Bits	356

IT'S NOT STRESS
THAT KILLS US,
IT IS OUR REACTION
TO IT.

HANS SELYE

WHERE DO WE START?

The origins of the stressed caveman, followed by 'The Caveman Principles'.

What does this book have to do with palaeoanthropology? Not one tiny bit of it. But it has everything to do with making you happier by understanding stress, communicating more effectively, and creating personal change, especially for the modern Caveman.

Academics are going to hate this book. Luckily, it was not written for them; it was crafted for you, the modern Caveman. The explanations within this book do not go too deep; they are created with enough information and examples to help you pick up useful tools for everyday life, mixed with a smidgen of humour.

If you are of the female persuasion, please don't let the title put you off. 'Caveman' has been a generic term for a long time, and the name covers both sexes. This book was not necessarily for 'him indoors'.

It was written for all modern Cavepeople.

Full disclosure: it has been written by a bloke. There was a little female influence, but it has been published for everyone to enjoy.

There is no complex mathematics to worry about and no final exam (unless you ask for one). Although there will be some anthropology, the study of human behaviour, it will be buried within the pages of this book, and I promise it will be covered painlessly.

This book was written to address a massive gap in the self-help sector. It offers a simple, easy-to-read solution to modern-day problems wrapped in a heart-written Caveman theory to help the masses.
Now that I have set the tone for this book, a simple, straightforward, humorous read, I hope you enjoy it.

As with any book, I have a website:
www.carljones.org
For those who want to learn more and to test your knowledge:
www.elevatedtraining.org

USING THIS BOOK

This book was written to give you what you want - a more straightforward and better life!

Its contents were created just for you, so scribble in the margins, fold down corners of the pages, and rip out the good stuff. This book and the website have been put together to help you understand and reduce your stress levels, provide a system to help you talk to people, get what you want from them, and give you a process to make positive changes in your life.

If you want to read this book from cover to cover, have fun. However, if you are a dip-in-and-out reader, I have divided it into three parts to make it easier.

If you:
- have trouble switching off
- difficulty in letting things go
- always feel wound up
- wanting some form of release
- need to know how to live a less-stressed life

...then you need Part 1. Here, you will find simple explanations for identifying stress. Stage one, identify it; stage two, deal with it. You need to know about the good stuff and the bad.

If you want:
- better relationships (at work, home or in friendships)
- have better rapport and interactions with others
- know how to deal with difficult people
- know why you act in specific ways
- to get an understanding of why people act differently

...then skip to Part 2. This is where you will find out which tribe you belong to. Read and learn how to identify the other tribe members and how you can interact and communicate with them better.

If you:
- are going through a challenging time at work or home
- have a personal goal you want to stick to
- want to try something different
(to make it happen)
- need to make an adjustment in your life
(the easy way)
- are feeling resistance to doing something unfamiliar
- need to understand what to do to make change happen

Then, the last section, Part 3 of this book, is for you. Change is never easy, especially when it is thrust upon you, but you can learn how to talk to your inner caveman and discover how to steer his pet, Mammoth. Resistance to change can be a thing of the past.

Ultimately, it does not matter if you want to read the whole book, but stage one is the recognition of stress. This is covered first because you have to identify stress before you can tackle it, or you can leave the book on a shelf collecting dust, but it will always be there when you need it.

THE CAVEMAN PRINCIPLES

You are the only one with the power to make a difference in your life. It took years of pain and a rewrite of this book, updating it and adding fresh content, to get it in your hands. This was something I had to do. What are you going to do?

If you decide to share your story with me, I'd love to hear it. Hopefully, it will be about how this book helped you. Email me at carl@carljones.org.
I genuinely hope you find the content useful. I wish you all the health and happiness.

Think 'Caveman'. www.elevatedtraining.org

THE GREATEST WEAPON

AGAINST STRESS

IS OUR ABILITY

TO CHOOSE ONE THOUGHT

OVER ANOTHER.

WILLIAM JAMES

PART ONE
I.
THE ORIGINS OF STRESS

There are Good and Bad Stressors.

"It's called 'stress' — It'll help with natural selection."

Stress is a daily human response; it is nothing more and nothing less than our human make up. Accept it as part of modern living, regardless of what others tell you. Complications arise when we forget this fact, and we end up making things far too complicated in an attempt to be less stressed; it is comical.

Stress is our body's natural reaction to an unexpected event or when facing a challenging time; this is when it kicks in. Most people try to ignore stress or believe they know everything there is to know about it, but then they have no control over it.

This section will give you an understanding, one you may not have been aware of, and with this new knowledge, you will begin to gain control.

We have all had our fair share of stress, but what is stress? Where does it come from, and what does it do to us? Some people know how stress affects them and can sense when it builds up. They seem to be able to do something about it before it is too late (we may hate these 'Zen' masters). You know of the ones that I mean, they always have a 'hippy' comment to make, whereas we'd rather throw a chair at someone's head and hand in our resignation rather than accept help to calm ourselves.

I'm guessing you are reading this book because you want a less stressful life. You are probably stressed right now, and this is what we will call the bad stuff. You will need help dealing with it.

Stress is caused every week, every day, every hour and every minute, but we may not be aware of it building up. The biggest problem with stress is that we no longer accept what it was designed to do for us. We no longer give it the respect it deserves.

The effects of harmful stress should never be underestimated; it can cause illness, destroy friendships, ruin marriages and cause long-term mental health issues to the unfortunate few.

Bad stress is a real problem; it has more impact on our lives than anyone could admit to. Stress cannot be seen, held, touched, measured, or predicted by others. Although people say they are 'stressed', at the time, no one knows what the full impact will be. Most people ignore it, deny being stressed, or even wear it as a badge of honour until it is too late. These people do not know how this stress reaction was caused and what it means in the long term. More importantly, they will not be interested in learning about it. They won't apologise. Instead, they make excuses and will see an apology as a weakness, that is, until this book was written and forced into their hands.

Stress reactions can be traced to one incident or a combination of many events with a trigger incident. Most people may need to learn what triggered the reaction. They may have done the same task a hundred times before, but it caused them to react on that one occasion.

These stress reactions have probably happened many times but have been ignored and not addressed, and then that one time it happens, all hell breaks loose. It will be worse than the other times, unmanageable, and may cause them to want to start tearing the place apart and anyone else who gets in their way. Overall, it makes no sense, but anyone with the help of this book can see why this occurs.

Let's start by explaining the stress response. Don't worry; this is not a biology lesson; no talk of blood or guts, and no cutting up frogs—simple biology 101, pure and simple. Stress is a word used to describe when our body feels an imminent attack threatening it. Our body is hardwired to deal with threats; it is an instinct kicking in; unless we can recognise it and stop the internal programming, we have no choice but to go along for the stress reflex ride.

To show another version of stress, ask yourself this question: have you ever been speaking to someone and been so engrossed in the conversation that when someone walks up beside you and says hello, it sets off an uncontrolled reaction?

You jump, your heart races, and you can't think straight. You've been spooked! You were six feet in the air and wanted to run for the hills. You can remember the fright for some time; these feelings are easy to recall.

You were probably clutching your chest, catching your breath before you realised you were not in danger, but what danger? What made you react like this?

I bet you have no idea why you reacted; you just shrugged and laughed it off, probably never giving it a second thought. Please think about it. This was your body getting ready to push the button.

What about a more serious situation? Have you ever been thrown into a life-or-death scenario, finding extraordinary strength to do something courageous? Have you ever saved your own life or that of another? Maybe, like me, you faced someone with a gun. Or were you crossing a road and never saw the car racing towards you? Somehow, before you knew it, you were standing somewhere completely safe, scenario over and situation under control.

There are extreme cases of people using their stress reflexes and getting reported in the news or even posted on YouTube. The ones that get shared a million times, as people watch in astonishment, even asking if it was fake. Documented examples are shared worldwide and constantly pop up on someone's newsfeed. These extraordinary feats only happen because people push their buttons.

These incredible responses are termed 'hysterical strength'. Incidents of mothers lifting cars off their children who were trapped underneath, people jumping from one building to the next to escape a fire, and even adults fighting off a fully grown polar bear to save schoolchildren are all studied.

Whether you were just spooked or need to find the strength and courage to fight a hungry bear, it all comes from the same reaction: pressing the stress button.

Stress buttons are subconsciously pushed when we need the 'fight or flight' response. Everyone has probably heard the phrase, but let's discover its origins.

The expression regularly pops up in conversation when people talk about scary experiences.

Knowing where stress comes from and what it does to the body is the first step in addressing daily stress levels.

First, we must get the word 'stress' out of the naughty bin; not all stress is bad. There is the good stuff, such as when someone needs to lift a car off someone or jump large distances to save their own life. These extreme reactions are all stress-related. Our body does what is necessary without being asked; it is designed to operate like this.

We can sometimes summon the need for more of the 'good' stress when we need a little extra boost, focus or concentration. As in the movies, when sweat is dripping, someone needs a steady hand to cut the red wire. In real life, such as an exam, needing clear thoughts and memory recall, or in a race, a little extra strength could be the difference between first and second place. This boost is when we convince our body that we need something extra.

Accessing the good stress, known as the Eustress response (moderate or normal psychological stress interpreted as beneficial), allows people to reach new or higher goals. Having a positive mindset massively helps. Anyone can do it with practice. When we push ourselves to achieve a goal, we create that extra stress, a self-managed condition that triggers the button.

When we achieve Personal Bests or better results, we put it down to hard work and dedication and then struggle to reproduce those results. Recognising that our bodies are responding to the perfect stress request, pushing the stress button helps get us there. Enough of the good stuff; we must deal with the bad stuff, which is why you bought this book—the stuff of nightmares. The negative stress is when we have no control over the button; people do not ask for it to be pressed, and in today's world, why do so many people need help? The bad stress is why we overreact, eat unhealthy stuff, shout, lose it, use alcohol, or want to curl up somewhere and be left alone. It's horrible because it can take hold anytime, and shaking this off feels impossible. The good news is that this book is here to help you understand this behaviour.

It sucks! One of our body's significant life-saving reactions can make us heroes one minute and villains the next. For me, that is precisely what happened. Throughout human history, our natural body's reaction has put some great leaders in charge when we needed them. Stress is responsible for leading others into the deepest, darkest crevices of their human psyches, even when they should be leading the country.

Bad stress gets daily recognition. It is the cause of all our problems; we all have it, and no one should feel alone. The same incident could occur to several people, each with a different reaction. One individual could be nonplussed, while another needs a week off work. It depends on the personality, mindset, emotional state, even upbringing, and current lifestyle of the person. It comes from various places, including lifestyle changes, dealing with annoying people, and work and home pressure.

When we experience bad stress, we do not know how to handle it. When we hear someone else is struggling with the bad stuff, they probably don't know how to handle it, and we don't know how to be the friend they need to guide them out of it.

It's usually handled by friends telling us to 'man up, buttercup'. These are not the friends we need and are not to be trusted to give advice or be asked for support.

When the source of stress is ignored and not tackled, people wallow in self-pity. The impact that prolonged stressful situations have on our bodies is immeasurable. The mishandling of stressful situations can cause a perfectly healthy person, who has a natural body reaction, to manifest into illness, including physical and mental pain.

There is an answer: get back control. From now on, we will stop thinking of it as bad. It is just a reaction, and we will start treating it with the respect it deserves.

Starting with a primary human reaction, 'fight, flight, or freeze', which comes after the button is pushed, these reactions contribute significantly to our everyday stress. Understanding our stress is a great place to start.

2.
FIGHT, FLIGHT OR FREEZE
HOW DID A CAVEMAN GET STRESSED?

Stress is a natural response, but what we do with it counts. As it is a result of the button being pressed, its original use was for the 'fight or flight' response, but modern living has added the 'freeze'. The fight or flight reaction, the lifesaving element that our Caveman ancestors developed, has now been ruined by modern-day living.

When cavemen started walking on two feet, and both sexes had far too much hair, they needed a backup, so they kept and developed the internal emergency button, using their animal ancestry as their guide.

They lived in tribes and were the food choice for many bigger, stronger animals. They were easy to catch and had just enough meat to make them a worthwhile lunch option.

Relying on natural pack instincts, Cavemen lived together, hunted together, and did things that made them less vulnerable. When the tribe stood together, they were not as easy a target for some animals. In their short years, their experience and ingenuity were passed on, allowing them to train others, grow, and live in relative safety.

Tribes made them strong. They lived and breathed each other's victories and failures. As a group, they fed their young and cared for the injured simultaneously. They would ensure that the tribe members were fit and healthy and that all had enough food. Due to their lifestyle changes, the button was being used less and less. It was needed because when they were caught unaware, it gave them extra strength and speed when required.

The caveman developed the button away from the original animal's needs. I may have promised no Biology lesson, but this next bit is important.

This 'button' is essentially the adrenal glands. These sit on top of the kidneys. When the brain believes it could be endangered or placed in a dangerous situation, it can activate the amygdala (our central processing unit for emotions). Lots of things happen, but the response we need when we are threatened is that the amygdala in the brain activates the glands in the kidneys. In the glands, the medulla, or the 'button', produces adrenaline, which helps the body do some genuinely outstanding and unexpected things.

Back in the caveman's day, this button would do one of two things, and our two new friends, Bert and Errol, will help explain it. Bert is a ferocious and brilliant Hunter. He always brings home the meat for his tribe. Bert leaves the cave in a Hunter pack. They all carry some weapons and spend days hunting their prey. They laugh and joke while working and feel relaxed roaming the land.

They start to track a Mammoth. These are bigger than today's modern elephants and much more dangerous. By himself, Bert knows that he does not stand a chance, but as a pack, he has every chance of bringing home enough meat to feed the entire tribe for weeks.

Until a point when Bert would have been enjoying the company of his fellow Hunters, his only thought has been to concentrate on finding his next meal. Then the Mammoth appears, and his attitude changes. Bert sneaks up closer, and as he approaches the mammoth, he suddenly starts to focus and feels different. Some short-term changes are going on. His body needs protection from all the crazy stuff he is about to do. He feels an excited fizz growing as the amygdala assesses the situation. His focus becomes pinpointed on the Mammoth. These feelings grow stronger as he gets closer to his prey.

The situation had changed, and Bert's actions activated his button, helping him transform from an everyday carefree Caveman to a hardened hunter focused on the job.

Experience will be involved, but using his button plays an important part. Pressing his button will give him extra focus, strength, quicker reactions, and speed. Now, with his band of hunters unconsciously doing the same, they are ready to kill the Mammoth. Bert's body needs to be hyper-reactive. His mind should be clear of everything but the Mammoth.

He should be extra alert, watching and waiting for the unknown, and able to respond within a second's notice to whatever comes his way.

Bert's brain has recognised a 'kill or be killed' scenario and is ready. It is being threatened with danger; even though it is Bert's conscious decision to be there, there is still a push of the button. That tiny gland sat on his kidneys, injecting adrenaline into Bert's body.

Bert's muscles and limbs come alive and are ready for action. The button has also pumped many other nasty toxins into his body, all designed to make his reasoning and reactions razor-sharp. These toxins start an internal chemical reaction, helping focus his mind. It can clear his body of unwanted waste and do odd things, such as making his skin extra sensitive and his hearing becoming selective. His heart rate rises, pumping blood around his body and into his limbs, ready to feed his muscles when needed. Bert's eyes have widened, allowing the detection of the slightest movement, down to the finest of detail; thoughts of his family, his 'to-do' list and how he looks in his new loincloth have been purged from his mind.

Bert's mind and body are ready for the fight. A button push has turned him from any everyday bloke into a single-minded, focused, super-strong killing machine. Bert knows he is not alone; all the other Hunters are with him, ready to strike, and this helps his body react to the fight response.

They can all run at superfast speeds, jumping higher, swinging harder, and reacting quicker. Because of their button, they can work harder together and overpower the Mammoth. They stop only when the beast is dead and the dust has settled. The hunters can relax again only when they have achieved their goal.

The push of their buttons delivered all the adrenaline and toxins they needed; it helped them win the fight. The fight would have used up all the secretions, having been burnt off through fierce exercise. All those nasty toxins used to focus the mind are now depleted. They can return to their normal carefree Caveman-style. They would probably feel sore, battered, and bruised, but those temporary superpowers have gone.

Exhausted by their prize, they drag what they can back to the cave, feeling proud of themselves and their achievement. They are completely spent, with nothing left, and they need to rest before their next hunt.

The fight-or-flight button has another use. Bert's brother, Errol, will help to demonstrate. He likes to wander off from the cave by himself. He enjoys collecting berries and other valuable items, like sticks (for when the tribe discovers fire).

Now Errol is happily pushing through the bushes and undergrowth, picking the ripest of berries and thinking of nothing. Besides the warm sunshine on his back, he has nothing to worry about and is at complete peace. He pulls back a bush and finds himself face-to-face with a Mammoth. He has no spear and no team of hunters around him. His brain kicks in, knowing that his life is in danger.

Errol's subconscious brain immediately recognises the threat, and his amygdala kicks in. It pushes the fight-or-flight button, his adrenal gland swings into action, and just like Bert when he faces his Mammoth, Errol is ready. The difference is that this Mammoth was unexpected.

Errol was unprepared, had no team or weapons, and needed a different response.

Errol's body has the same adrenaline and toxins squirt as Bert's scenario. That jet of fluids into his system gives his brain a fraction of a second to respond, readying his reflexes to become strong and agile. His mind clears and focuses on survival; it provides the fright response, and the flee command is given. Muscles are already primed, his speed from standing still to full sprint is beyond his standard achievement, his brain forgets about berries and strange brown things, and it is focused and providing crystal clear thinking. He can instantly see the planned escape route. His body and mind are working in unison, and there is no external thinking to influence or lower the decision.

Without thinking for himself, Errol is already on his toes. He automatically drops everything that is going to slow him down. Already at full speed, sprinting away from the threat of the Mammoth, Errol has a chance to get away before the Mammoth can think about doing anything.

Errol runs back to the cave, and when he gets there, he is exhausted but elated that he is still alive. His running and mental focus have been burning away all those toxins and adrenaline squirted into his system. He will need time to recover and will take the rest of the day off before he goes back out looking for anything useful.

Errol and Bert's bodies used up everything provided by the push of their stress buttons. They both live to see and fight another day. They know the risks they face the next time they go out and must be recovered and ready. They will take the time to heal properly and then be reset, ready to do it all again.

The fight or flight button is still active, a life-saving tool. It ensured Bert and Errol, our Caveman ancestors, could survive in the brutal world they knew back then, but the world has changed. These stress buttons are still being pressed in the modern day, but we have developed different lives that may not need these responses, but we are stuck with them.

We may be taller, less hairy, and have better dental care, but most of our internal organs, gizmos, and thingamabobs are still the same, including the 'fight or flight' button. Instead, we have meddled with nature's gift, and due to our hectic lifestyles, we have had to create a freeze response. This is now the core issue of our daily stress.

3.
LOOK OUT FOR STRESS MAMMOTHS

Modern-day Cavemen.

We were never built for modern-day society. Over the last 50 years, we have seen more innovation and change than in the entire history of mankind. Until then, we had quite a few millenniums to adjust to a transformation. People have had to find new ways to live, socialise, work, travel and play in the blink of an eye. Our bodies have not had a chance to evolve that quickly, so we have had to make it up as we went along and have had to force it upon ourselves to survive. If we could ask for some body upgrades from Evolution, we could do with Bluetooth or a USB socket and a charging port somewhere handy. We have not even been able to get rid of the unsightly back hair most men have... or worked out what the appendix does, surely we would have gotten rid of it by now? These adjustments take time.

In today's world, most of us live in negative, fear-driven, and even numbing environments. This type of lifestyle is the norm. As time passes, it gets harder to smile, and we choose to call this "being an adult," but all of us would like the opportunity to go on the playground swings again.

Living busy, hectic lifestyles, we tell ourselves lies. We could plan fun things for the weekend or a great time for a holiday, but we end up using the time for sleeping and recovering, ready to restart our adult jobs the following Monday.

We know what life we would like to have, but we don't stop to question our treadmill existence; we accept it and get on with life. Accepting that society needs us to do this to become part of the numbing system, we put up with it and are willing to adopt the new ideals, even though they are against nature's wishes. These negative emotions become part of our lifestyle; bad events happen to us, and we accept that this is our 'life'.

This may sound a little melodramatic and a 'woe is me' type tale, but it has a point; most people reading this book probably feel this way, and there is good news. This is why I wrote this book. This condition indicates that we are unaware of how to manage our stress button.

We have unknowingly allowed stress to creep into our daily lives, and instead of it serving its proper purpose, it has dug in and camped out, making us feel stretched and ineffective.

Most people are probably unaware that there is constant negativity and that it is a terrible environment. We believe words such as being 'driven' mean that we should burn ourselves out to get there. We believe that to have a good life, we must do this to ourselves. We become numb to joy and give up our freedom to live a life we never seem to achieve.

We accept that if we want nice things, people are allowed to mistreat us and that we can do the same to others. What a nasty and vicious cycle modern Cavemen have gotten themselves into.

That got heavy very quickly! Sorry if that was too strong, but some messages don't hit hard enough. A slap around the face with a wet fish is better than being told everything is OK whilst sitting on a beach enjoying the view, ignoring the tidal wave coming right at you.

I wanted to make this book a light and easy read, but sometimes, it must get to the point. Those last few paragraphs were written to make you sit up and take stock. If they didn't, please reread them. We are guilty of letting our lives drift by (me included), and only when someone points it out do we realise what has been happening.

It's a good job that I will only do this in this chapter; the rest of the book is all positive stuff. At least there isn't any complicated maths stuff that usually goes into these types of books.

Back to the negativity, how many ways do we describe damaging human emotions using English? Believe it or not, this list is growing, new words to describe new ways to torment ourselves about it. The dictionary believes there are roughly 560 different words that we can use to tell someone how we are feeling.

My old work colleagues thought I had the emotional depth of a teaspoon. It may be useful to be referred to as an article that makes a cup of tea, but with hindsight, this is not a good comparison to be proud of.

This might be a small insight into a bloke's mind for my female readers. Many other blokes and I believe things are good or bad, and there is no middle ground. Blokes are either happy or 'busy'. This sets out the range of emotions that most men typically want to share.

However, if you are into linguistic sentiment analysis, the dictionary believes that out of those 560 emotions, 345 describe a negative one, such as sadness, sorrow, depression or upset. The mathematicians have worked out that there are only 215 to tell the good ones, like being happy, joyful, and satisfied. I did not separate the neutral emotions, such as "OK", from the positive emotions because, as stated above, a bloke's response is good or bad.

Trusting my maths, 62% of our emotional, descriptive words describe our negative feelings. There are almost twice as many ways to express the bad ones in our lives than we can use to focus on the good.
Leaving 38% of these words to describe good feelings and emotions, it's no wonder we live in a negative state. Finding a word to describe that mindset is much easier.

We love to complain; without knowing it, we have been subjected to numerous daily TV soap operas, access to car crash documentaries, or feeling jealous from watching real-life rich people live their lives on their TV series. These give us ammunition to continue making ourselves feel bad about our purpose. People have been conditioned to need their serialised drama input, with writers competing against each other to make the next storyline the 'worst' possible. Without knowing it, people watch constant cliffhangers and see others act out their pain. It doesn't stop there as people relive it at work or on social media, gossiping about the latest episode while guessing the future plot line. There is no release from the tension and negativity; it just sits there, and we fall into the trap of watching it, becoming part of our daily routine.

Compared to horror movies (which I hate), these might mess with your moral compass, but scientists suggest they can boost your immune system and make you feel better. After a jolt from a scary scene, the mind returns to a calm state, and then the brain releases the feel-good hormones dopamine and serotonin. It is all over, and although you might have a few nightmares, the negativity has already dispersed, and there is no constant negative drip feed.

People probably don't even enjoy the suspense of a 'good' soap drama, but it is just an addiction to daily input. As we are no longer consciously in control of what we are doing to our emotions, it is time we take stock of things.

It is not just the soaps; society lives in a negative state. There is a constant need for a news feed. It can be read or watched live, anytime, and anywhere. As there is a demand, agencies have provided a solution. Numerous 24-hour news stations, apps, news feeds, links in social media and the 'news chat' around the kettle at work. All reporting on negative national and international news stories has probably had no bearing or impact on us. Yet we sit and watch updates on terrible news stories happening on the other side of the world, out of our control. These constant negative ramblings are designed to do one thing: sell news; it is big business. News agencies understand society's needs and want to hear and see them, so they find the worst news stories to feed people's appetites. If there is nothing sinister going on for people to read about, some agencies will even create a concern and hope it sticks.

Blindly walking around in a hostile society is unhealthy. However, now that you can see the impact this has, you have a choice. You can feel better, switch off the soaps and don't watch or read the news. Concentrate on things you can control, such as your family, friends, and the neighbourhood. Go and chat with the neighbours and see how your mood changes.

Emotions and external influences significantly affect our ability to cope with stress. As modern cavemen, we still need the survival instinct. There are still times that we need that little 'extra' something. We need to be able to push our buttons when threatened, but as it is hard-wired, and our hectic lives blur the need, it can go off when we don't need it. When it misfires, something different to the fight or flight instinct happens.

We have never been able to evolve to anything better, and the button is still in daily use. We can use it with the same reactions as our ancestors did when they faced their Mammoths; everything works the same way. Our brains have the same access to the amygdala (the emotional CPU) and adrenal glands that shoot out the toxins pumped into our bodies.

The only difference between us and the Caveman is that our society has changed, and the threat from a Woolly Mammoth might have been removed. But are they truly extinct? A misguided belief in their extinction has caused us to believe we no longer need the original reflexes, but in doing this, we have had to add a new reflex, the 'freeze' reaction. The modern-day caveman now has the same button, but it services the 'fight, flight, and freeze' responses.

Talking about these Mammoths, you may still think that there are no longer any threats from them today. I'm afraid I must disagree as the threat of a 'metaphorical' Mammoth is still present; they can produce the same fight or flight response as they always have. They make us want to push our buttons, and there are plenty of Mammoths still out there that we encounter every day. We interact with them at work, at home, and when socialising. No one knows they are there; they are hiding in plain sight.

The more critical element is that we have chosen to ignore our Mammoths because society has taught us that we are no longer allowed to use the 'fight or flight' reflex. We are taught from childhood to consider another response; combined reasoning has produced the 'freeze' reaction.

You are probably scratching your head, thinking I have lost the plot, but think about it. We have the same button, handed down from the Cavemen, the same one that Bert and Errol used to save their lives in the last chapter.

We still feel a sudden rush of adrenaline and fear. Those feelings and reactions would have been very similar to those Bert and Errol had when they came face to face with a real six-ton Woolly Mammoth. So, why can we still push the button if there are no Mammoths?

Modern-day Mammoths trigger the same response when we feel threatened by them. They need to be more sneaky, as these Mammoths are not out in the open. We must hunt them; it is a mammoth-eat-mammoth world out there; otherwise, they will find us.

Tip: Read this next section using Sir David Attenborough's voice.

Today's Mammoths are at home, especially when we are at work; they can be found everywhere, and they are there to challenge us. They have developed the use of camouflage better than any animal has ever managed to master. They are champion hiders, choosing only to appear when they decide to before their prey. Their job is done when they have scared the living daylights out of their victims. They disappear back into the foreground, leaving the recipient human scared and acting irrationally.

Other humans nearby will not have seen this Mammoth; it was a targeted attack. Bystanders will need more information and clarification on the emotional display that the targeted human is going through. They may think that the victim is being petty, that they are overreacting. As the response is out of character, they may be tempted to scold them "grow up", or worse "man up". The witnesses may smile and start to move away, making the Mammoth's attack even more impactful, leaving the sufferer alone and feeling more vulnerable. Other humans will see this as an opportunity to speak about this outburst around the kitchen area or over email, spreading the Mammoth's impact far and wide.

The Mammoth's pounce may only have been for a micro-second, causing its prey to hit its stress button when others would not have seen it. When we look for these Mammoths, it becomes easy if you know where to search. When trained, you will be able to see them everywhere. Then, it will be easier to know which ones are targeting you and identify other Mammoths lining up to deal with your colleagues.

Looking at a regular, modern-day Caveman's daily work routine, we can start to pick out the potential attacks. This unsuspecting victim works, does daily chores, speaks to clients, and gets on with the job. Then, out of the blue, a Mammoth appears right before them. No one else saw it coming. How did it manage to sneak up to its mark completely undetected?

The first inkling our stooge started to recognise it was when they heard the 'ping' from the laptop. A new email had landed in the inbox. They looked at the sender and saw it was from the big boss.

Opening the message, thinking it is another useless 'to everyone' email, they see the outline of the Mammoth. "Come and see me in my office ASAP."

There are no other email recipients; the rest of the message is blank. Staring at the email, only eight words, our Mammoth strikes. For a fraction of a second, the words form the shape of the Mammoth, and cold sweat and panic set in. It scares the pants off our worker.

There it is, the modern-day Mammoth. Showing itself, then disappearing into the air. Our victim has already subconsciously hit the stress button. Our negative outlook and lifestyle start to grind the gears, and expectations do the rest. Feeling flustered and without more information, they ask the person sitting next to them what they think the message means. The other person reads the exact eight words, shrugs and says, "Probably nothing," not seeing any trace of the Mammoth.

Our modern-day Caveman, who saw the Mammoth right before them, still feels threatened. Their minds and bodies are already reacting to the hit from the button.

Nothing spectacular has happened. Thinking this is some punishment coming via email, the mind has already gone down a rabbit hole.

The hostile world they are used to will ruin their day.

They have already suspected the worst; they're going to get fired. The threat feels natural; the button has been pressed. Our Caveman is the only one who saw this threat; they are the only ones who must deal with it.

We are all hardwired similarly; society and upbringing have conditioned us. Most of us are not used to being spoken to like this. "Nothing good will come from this" is the only thought process, and we immediately go to the worst-case scenario. It might not be such a big surprise any other day, especially if others are in the same boat. The Mammoth has been waiting for this moment to pounce; it took the opportunity. It jumped right in front of our poor, hard-working, distracted colleague and made them push their button. Other people may think this reaction is entirely irrational and unwarranted, but it did not happen to them; they do not have an email from the big boss, and the mammoth is not interested in them.

Our victim is sat at their desk, still staring at the words on the screen.

The push of the button has blown away all rational thought.

Our Caveman knows where this conversation is going, and they cannot comprehend it. Their brain has just had a massive injection of toxins, making them think of all the awful things that are going to happen, but there is nothing they can do about it.

The Mammoth does not care about the aftermath; it has no feelings on the matter, and its job is done. Our Caveman is left to deal with it alone, thinking that no one at work has ever paid them a compliment, so this must be bad news.

Like most work environments (apart from a few exceptional companies), people are too busy to praise someone for doing a good job. Some managers actively dissuade others from expressing gratitude; the "people are paid to work" attitude prevails. Our victim works at one of the not-so-good places, works hard, gets the job done to the best of their ability, and then goes home, believing they've done a good enough job to get paid.

THE CAVEMAN PRINCIPLES

The email triggered the button. The Mammoth popped up where the danger was thought to be. This gave our caveman insight into the boss's thoughts and led them to conclude that this would be a one-sided conversation.

Nothing good was going to come from this.

Over time, as in many places, there has been no positive work praise, only enforcement. People become used to expecting the worst. These interactions are easy to ignore until they happen to us. Now and again, our guard drops, and the Mammoth waits to show us the potential outcome. When it happens, our instinct tells us something is wrong; we have no information on the matter, and as natural worriers, we presume the severest outcome. In hostile environments, we prefer to discuss our negative interactions or other people's misfortunes. This is why we moan about any bad situations at work rather than all our good work.

Back to the email, our Caveman expects the worst. They get up and start to head towards the boss's door. They will go through everything they have done over the last three months, thinking, "What could I have done wrong?" and "Tonight, I'm going to have to rewrite my CV."

Halfway to the office, the adrenaline designed for the fight-or-flight reflex is already coursing through their veins. Due to social etiquette, they cannot lose control in the office, so they hold it. Muscles primed to run or kick out are painfully held back. Starting to feel hot, shaky, and about to faint, our worker feels these feelings getting stronger. The toxins make them feel sick, but as per their design, they are not being used up.

Due to the lack of information, a thousand thoughts are being processed at lightning-quick speeds, thanks to those toxins floating around, unable to focus the mind. By the time they get to the boss's door, they're a wreck, using all their willpower to make their legs work, moving forward instead of away. The forced reaction controls the internal panic; the fight or flight tries to get complete control. Our Caveman is on the verge of losing control of all emotions. Deep down, they want to either run away or start fighting, even if it is with the boss. If they succumbed to either desire, it would make the boss's job more manageable, and they would not get a chance to pack up their desk.

Instead, conditioning and expectations force them to stand and face the music.

Our Caveman croaks out, "You wanted to see me?" putting on a brave face and feeling the beads of sweat roll down their back. In the office, they are trapped, cornered, and have no idea what will happen next. The fight and flight is now screaming for control.

Many of us can relate to similar situations; for me, it was on the threshold of a Superintendent's office. The Mammoth is not working for the boss; it is just a nasty, vicious, selfish animal out to make us squirm and wants us to trigger our button response. Our brave Caveman holds it all in and waits. The boss looks up from the computer screen and leans forward, giving all the signs of a pre-emptive strike. The caveman waits a bit longer; all the time, the leg tremors get worse. The boss asks, "I need someone to help another department. They have more work than they can handle. How do you feel about taking on some of their work?"

The Caveman washes the question around in their frazzled brain. They're already stretched doing their job, but cannot process anything now.

They look for any danger signs, but they are still on edge. The penny drops, and they realise that they are not getting sacked. There is no chance of relaxing; the button has been pressed.

They need to shake it off and lie down, but all they can do is fight the urge to run. Their head is trying to process the question and provide a decent answer, but there is nothing but haze and confusion.

Those toxins and a burst of adrenaline are surging around their body, needing to be used up. Unable to unpress the button, they are sat there unable to do anything. Running or fighting will get rid of those nasty pollutants in their body. No longer needed, these are left floating around in their bloodstream. Nothing can calm their heart rate; sweating is getting worse, and the refocus in their brain is out of order. They should be saying that they are snowed under with all their work and that the last job still needs their full attention, but they cannot get out of the office without an answer. They cannot formulate any other response except "Of course". The boss smiles, pointing at the door. The audience is over.

THE CAVEMAN PRINCIPLES

Our exhausted Caveman jumps out of the chair and walks out, trying to work out what just happened. They have too much work already and just accepted more because they could not think of a reason to say no. They feel cheated, and all because of the Mammoth.

First, they were scared by the appearance of the Mammoth, leading them to believe they were about to get sacked, which led them to press the button. As the focus was on how they could keep their jobs, the button was pressed, and the boss unknowingly used this opportunity to give them extra work. No fight. No excuses. No reasoning.

Back at their desk, the person beside them asks if they are all right. The caveman is exhausted and angry, but they have no idea why, so they say, "Yeah, I'm OK."

They sit there and boil for a few minutes, getting angry and emotional. They feel stupid and hate everyone, including the boss, but this is all the Mammoth's fault. It is not stupidity; it is the Mammoth laughing at them, and it burns.

This is the last opportunity for our Caveman to release. Sat in a chair, fuming, never needing those toxins and adrenaline boost, it remains in their system. These ingredients need to be used but have been suppressed. The body must dissolve those harmful fluids into the soft tissues and organs where they are stored, never to be used for their intended purpose.

Controlling our buttons is difficult. A Zen master dedicates their waking life to not getting stressed, but they do not have a 9-5 job, kids, a life, and a mortgage. We leave ourselves open to being tricked and abused by our Mammoths, which happens far too often. The good news is that you have already made progress. You are reading this book and will start to understand the button issue.

Primed for another Mammoth attack, our Caveman is having a terrible day at work. They have just picked up more work and want to go home. In the car, driving home, defences are already low, but this drive should be an easy one. It has been done hundreds of times before. It is usually a time for reflection, a chance to unwind, but they are wound tighter than an eight-day clock.

THE CAVEMAN PRINCIPLES

Coming up to some traffic, they are used to the dual carriageway—a line of cars already in front of them. Slowing down and joining the back of the queue, their junction is coming up. Feeling the tension from the day, the traffic is slow progress, but once off the main road, it is a short, easy drive home.

Another Mammoth has been watching, reading the situation, and waiting for the best moment. Then, bang, it strikes when the modern-day caveman is about to come off at the junction. These pesky blighters are masters of disguise and are not seen until the last minute. It came out of nowhere and took our caveman by surprise. They just wanted to get home, but that did not stop the mammoth from making them push their button again.

This time, the Mammoth is in full view in the back window of a red BMW. It decided to push its ugly mug up against the BMW glass for a moment, just as the BMW squeezed into the gap that was far too small for it but right in front of our Caveman's car. The Mammoth appears to be working with the BMW driver this time, but it is just there for the ride. The BMW decided not to queue up. It drove down the outside lane and pushed in, at the last minute, right in front of our Caveman's car.

The Caveman, already on edge from the day's shenanigans, has no mental capacity or strength to stop the button from being pressed. It's too late; the fight-or-flight response has already started.

There is no choice for our Caveman in a little car. An inconsiderate driver has threatened them. They slam on the brakes to stop hitting the BMW as it swerves in front of them, with no sign of thanks. The entitlement of the BMW driver is clear, and the button is pressed. More adrenaline and toxins have been pumped into our caveman's system, but they are powerless to use it for the intended purpose. This might be a different scenario, but the outcome is the same as the last; they invoke the freeze response.

They need to use up that adrenaline. Their body wants them to do something with it: get out of the car, run up to the BMW, and start fighting with the driver, but that is unacceptable in today's society. You can be cut up in traffic but not kick a bumper.

Our Caveman sits there, stewing, strapped in by their seatbelt, gripping the steering wheel, their knuckles turning white. Their only activity is small hand stretches towards the BMW, which is insufficient to burn up those toxins in the body. These toxins need to be used, but are reabsorbed back into the body. Those harmful substances are stored alongside the unused toxins from all the previous button pressings, but will never be used.

Off the dual carriageway, our caveman has lost the BMW and has one last stop before they get home. They pop into the shop to pick up a pint of milk, ready for breakfast the following day. Finding the milk, everything is going smoothly. They are still riled from the BMW incident, but they are just chuntering and not raging any more.

Walking toward the eight items or less self-service tills, the queue is short. Finally, they can relax; they'll be home soon. Pulling a few coins from a pocket, they expect to be back in the car shortly.

In the background, another Mammoth is hiding, ready to hit them. Perhaps they are part of a WhatsApp group? This one is in the least expected places. Our caveman sees something odd. The person in front of them has nothing in their hands.

They have been holding a place in the queue for their partner, who has just arrived with a massive trolley. The mammoth strikes again, moving from under the trolley. Our caveman is being laughed at before it scampers off under the shelves. The Mammoth moves so fast that no one else sees it.

Already on edge, with no choice, our caveman's body is exhausted, with no control left. Seeing a Mammoth again so quickly and for the third time on the same day, the button is pressed again. They've lost their place in the queue to someone without the right to use it.

Bang! Their bodies are back in fight-or-flight mode, challenged again, and there is no release. The need to conform, to force themselves to react respectably, has almost gone.

The heart rate shoots up, and they feel hot and angry. They want to grab and shove that trolley out of the way, which will start a fight. Their body wants it to happen and is ready for it. There is a need to run forward and jump in front of these impolite shoppers; instead, they start rocking on the balls of their feet.

Their button tells them to do all these things, and their mind goes through a thousand intelligent sayings. However, they are fighting the desire, being taught that society will not tolerate these shopping indiscretions, but one day, they know they will not be able to fight it. Swallowing hard, our caveman waits and pays for the milk before leaving. The milk might end up in an orifice on another day, but not today.

It was close, but their reasoning saved them from being banned from the shop. They sit safely in their car, reabsorbing those last toxins into the body, and watch the couple unload their trolley into a car parked in front of them. Biting their tongue and feeling a massive urge to do something, they force themselves to drive away.

Every mammoth leaves a mark, and it hurts. There was a build-up throughout the day, and it almost got messy. As our Caveman drove away, they screamed, "Why me?" There was no other physical exertion to burn off any adrenaline; they just had to reabsorb those toxins.

These are just a few examples of where these blasted mammoth critters hide and how they watch and work out their next victims, but there are many more. Mammoths can find thousands of places to hide; our modern-day caveman must always be alert. They are everywhere: letters from the tax man, personal emails, and the "Sorry we missed you" cards in the letterbox. Most might be ignored, but when one gets through, they tear down all defences to allow others to follow.

Hiding places are designed by the Mammoth. They wait for their prey for days, weeks, even months, letting you see them just as you remember you should have taken the chicken out of the freezer or in the blue lights when you are forced to remember your brake light is no longer working. They disappear as quickly as they arrive, leaving a trail of damage and pain in their wake.

These mammoths have had years of practice. They know when we are vulnerable, striking when our guard is down and hitting us at the optimal time. They force us to push the button and then rub salt in the wound. Afterwards, we can always feel their presence, feel them watching us and laughing. They want us to lose control. Instead of using the fight-and-flight response, we use the freeze response and fight the imaginary mammoth.

4.
DON'T PUSH THE BUTTON
HOW CAN YOU STOP IT?

Everyone loves a great story, and to show you how to stop pushing your button, we have an ex-soldier showing us where the Mammoths hide and how to avoid them. Once, an ex-soldier lived in a modest home on a beautiful beach. He had a fulfilling life, a loving family, and a small fishing boat. He loved to fish, and every day, he woke up happy. Each day, he would get into his boat and go to sea, searching for tuna. He became so good that on every trip, he brought back enough tuna to feed his entire family and have extra to sell at the local market. He would catch, feed, and trade his fish, making more than enough money to buy the things he needed to have a comfortable and good lifestyle.

One day, an Investor walked past a fisherman's market, and they saw the catch of tuna. The Investor asked about the ex-soldier's story, where he lived, and his knowledge about catching such beautiful fish. The Investor knew that with this fisherman's ability and skill, he could make some serious money.

Speaking with the fisherman, the investor offered a chance to work with him. The Investor stated that he was a business expert with a second-to-none education. He boasted that his business sense would allow the fisherman to grow a business quickly. With the Investor's capital, he could be running an entire fleet of fishing boats, catching beautiful tuna every day. This ex-soldier could be hauling vast amounts of fish and earning larger sums of money, from which they would share the bounty.

The investor continued that if the man were prepared to work long hours, with the investor advising him, he would one day earn enough money to retire. The ex-soldier could then hang up his fishing gear, buy a house along the beach, and do whatever he enjoys. The then-retired ex-soldier would have enough money to feed his family and be able to relax whenever he wanted to.

The ex-soldier smiled and asked if the Investor's education was expensive. The Investor grew by a few inches and stated that it had cost his father a lot of money. Slightly intrigued, the Investor asked, "Why do you ask about my education?"

The man replied, "No reason, as it is probably too late to ask for a refund."

This story shows how some people are willing to exploit others, offering what people might want to hear but not what they need. Our ex-soldier was smart enough to know when he had enough and did not need to be introduced to more mammoths. Regardless of the promise or outcome, only some offers or opportunities will suit us. With every opportunity, there is risk and, therefore, stress. Our greed and today's speed of life make it hard to spot, but quite a few Mammoths are lurking within this story. We start by looking to see what we currently have and what we will gain from the opportunity. Like any risk, we must be prepared to gamble, "stick" or "twist."

Mammoths probably appeared as soon as the ex-soldier considered the Investor's offer. The Investor genuinely believed he could help the ex-soldier and would not have intended any Mammoth attack.

Our ex-soldier knew that his life was complete. He did not take the bait to 'improve' his life and did not see the need to do anything that would set his button off. He did not jump at the offer to become a wealthy fisherman. He was comfortable with his life and could control the urge to make an irrational decision and gamble. Instead, he decided to bypass those pesky Mammoths.

The Investor was not thinking about what the ex-soldier wanted and was unaware he would drop a herd of Mammoths into his life. He probably only thought he would be helping this poor man when he saw an opportunity to use his skills. The Investor asked the wrong question: Who wants to fish daily in a tiny boat? Instead, he should have asked if the ex-soldier was happy and if he wanted to change his life.

He thought he should be rewarded for trying to help this ex-soldier, whether he needed it or not. A point to note: not everyone sees wealth as having access to lots of money. If greed gets in the way, we put money before happiness, as the Investor did in this story. Our ex-soldier did not want the stress of building a business to get what he had already.

Individuals can disregard other people's thoughts and beliefs, rushing into doing something they consider worthy, when all they do is create hiding places for a Mammoth. Relating this to our narrative, we must slow things down and seriously consider our options. Are people helping or causing our stress and confusion? The best way to deal with a (un)helpful person is to be polite and not accept the offer, graciously decline, or come up with a one-liner, just like our ex-soldier.

Get comfortable saying "no." Only push ourselves when "we" want to, even if we believe people rely on us. It is OK to say no. Taking back this control will create more happiness and less opportunity for a Mammoth to attack.

Watching for modern-day Mammoths is not easy. Everyone can deal with a small number of stressors in their life. This is normal. When we hand the control to someone else, like a boss or a needy friend (or a greedy Investor), this is when the button is abused. Managing a manager is a skill; we will cover this in Part 2 of the book.

Lurking Mammoths hide in someone else's requests or best intentions. Remember, they only show themselves to their prey for a fraction of a second. Even the most sincere, kindest person can offer help, but we can face the wrath of an attack when we already feel the strain. A Mammoth pounce will trigger the unwanted response, the button press, and a torrent of upset toward their kindness. Mammoths like to prolong the pain, rubbing salt into the wounds, knowing an apology will be needed, to add embarrassment to the pain of a button push.

We can all bear some of the blame. A last-minute, quick one-liner email, poorly typed, is sent without a second thought. It can have people pushing their buttons. A simple sentence, maybe with no context or a typo, can easily hide a Mammoth. We are offering it a launch pad for a full-scale attack when others read it. Writing the email was a 'need to get it done' rather than a weighed and correctly executed action. Slow down. We are unaware that we attached the Mammoth, and we will blame the reader for 'reading it wrong', but end up in a no-win contest. The reader, being the only person to have seen the Mammoth, finds it hard to hear any justification, and they end up feeling hurt and misunderstood, while we, the writer of the email, feel things have been blown out of proportion. In the distance, a mammoth can be heard laughing, knowing it has a double whammy.

Every press of our button causes upset, taking valuable minutes and too much headspace from our already hectic day. It creates negative thoughts and requires us to regain control before moving on. Modern society teaches us that the freeze approach is expected over the fight-or-flight response. The freeze response is the most tiring and probably the main reason why society is struggling so much with anxiety and other mental health conditions.

The amount of effort that needs to be put into calming ourselves down is immense. No wonder we arrive home from work or, after a trip out, completely exhausted. It is no longer the nine hours we spend at work, focused on completing tasks, but constantly living through using our buttons. Things are getting more complicated, people more difficult to deal with, making us want to crash on the sofa and desperate for release. The constant pressing of our buttons causes us the fatigue we feel and the frustration we hold deep down.

At the end of a stressful day, life now is us not wanting to do anything other than sit in front of the TV or go to bed. Wouldn't it be good if we could change this? If the modern-day Cavemen from the previous chapter compared their number of presses of their button to Bert and Errol, it would easily be a multiple of the number, probably in the double figures. In comparison, Bert and Errol only pushed their buttons once or maybe twice a day and, more importantly, when they pushed their button, they were allowed to run around, burning off those toxins before taking a rest period.

Remember not to underestimate the power of the press. Each mammoth wants us to push it, which takes away control. With each press, future presses are easier to trigger. The strength needed to resist another push fades throughout the day, and as we tire from the constant Mammoth attacks, our moods and mindsets change. At home, our safe space, we have no energy left, and we can no longer prevent another push. We end up firing off at the wrong people. Our loved ones and friends get short shrift; all they did was ask a question. Each push causes our stress levels to rise, and each trivial situation becomes more stressful than the last.

Relationships fail, friendships are forgotten, and our home lives fall apart. Ultimately, a Mammoth's job gets easier and easier until it takes over your life and wins. When they win, we are talking about divorce, a new job, and having to start over, followed by therapy and recovery from sickness. Every button press is recorded as a stress 'event' in our bodies. Daily Mammoth sightings, attacks, and button-pushing all hit us, leaving a mark. We are so busy conforming to 'expected outcomes' that we ignore them and cannot learn how to prevent our buttons from being pressed. The compound effect kicks in; like a well-used light switch, less pressure is needed each time you use it before it finally breaks, and the light no longer works.

Button presses release adrenaline and other toxins. These are pumped into the body and should be used for immediate physical exertion. They were not designed to be stored in delicate tissues, which is unhealthy.

Our designed ability to survive needs our button, which is hardwired in; only natural evolution can change this. It is modern-day living that we must blame, and as this is the only thing we can change, it is within our power. The most significant change we can all make is to add a rest period to our day.

We all have contracts at work; we are allowed lunch breaks and rest time, and laws in the UK demand that computer users take regular screen breaks. But we choose not to take them, becoming martyrs at work and causing our self-destruction and illness. I and many others will almost guarantee that regular breaks will reduce button presses and diminish stress, and people will be happier. Managers must enforce these rest breaks; they will allow the body to calm down, making the next button press a little harder to push and making the person happier and even more productive. The human body is an amazing design; given time, rest, and support, it can repair itself and even deal with unwanted substances.

You are now nodding and yelling "Yes!" as you can relate to the constant pressing. What are you going to do about it? Because if you don't tackle it now, things will get worse. A medical condition called 'Chronic Stress' is horrendous, and no one wants that.

This illness can come from people who push their buttons far too often. Living with all that bad stuff in their systems for too long and without any rest periods is a recipe for disaster. The fact that you are reading this book means that you have recognised this and you are already looking at how to get rid of this 'stress'. The first step is to understand where and why we get stressed, and we have covered all of that. You have probably already started to plan changes in your life, avoiding mammoths and taking time outs.

It is essential to recognise that the stress toxins designed to save our lives are now slowly killing us because our lifestyle is not conducive to our fight or flight response. Muscles and organs have absorbed high doses of these harmful fluids for years and stored like nuclear waste, needing to be left alone for long periods to become safe. If we can manage these levels of toxins properly, then they can be expelled before they do any real damage. But if we keep adding to them, most of our organs and body tissue will be saturated, and it can slowly rot and destroy the healthy matter.

The body was not designed to absorb so many button hits in one day. Our busy, hectic lifestyle overloads our system and could be causing a mass build-up of toxins in our organs.

Evolution has not kept pace with us. Rush hour traffic and working in front of computer screens were never on the agenda, and no safety switch was considered.

In 2023, stress was one of the leading causes of many modern-day health problems. Numbers do not lie, as 13.7 million working days were lost in the UK (or £28.3 billion – checking the NICE report). 55% of workers feel that work is getting more intense and demanding. 60% of 18–24-year-olds and 41% of 25-34-year-olds feel pressured and stressed at work (MH Foundation). If this is not tackled now, it will become a complication in the future. Stress has been proven to prolong and worsen any illness. Stress has been linked to anxiety, overdrinking (alcoholism), depression, sleep disorders, and many other concerns.

There is a growing number of studies that suggest stress can cause early heart disease. It can aid or excel in the growth of cancerous cells, and there is no doubt that it can create blood pressure problems.

Looking up the research carried out by Cancer Research UK, the APA (American Psychological Association) and many more worldwide, they say stress is a ticking time bomb. There are hundreds of studies blaming stress for countless illnesses and conditions. People do not need to be medical students to know that stress is nasty; no one wants it, and everyone Is subject to it regardless of the life-damaging illnesses it is being linked to.

We know that stress can affect our appearance; it can make us sweat, produce greasy skin, cause acne and even early hair loss. I have often woken the day after a stressful event and found a huge spot on the end of my nose; I then check my hairline. It can also reduce and even kill a sex drive. Yep, you heard that right. There is no more coitus, rumpy-pumpy, or even being able to think about it.

Stress also messes with our emotions and our ability to communicate. Working through the freeze response makes a sufferer blinkered, focused on surviving, and unable to see the whole picture.

Spinning so many plates, watching everyone, only able to do just enough to prevent them from dropping.

When people ask or try to help, it is seen as interfering as we struggle to keep the plates spinning. We cannot explain anything to anyone and be able to hand over anything. Instead, we use more effort swatting away help rather than accepting it, pushing us deeper into a selfish zone of stress.

Stress is the most prolific culprit in a relationship's downfall because of its many negative factors. The lack of emotion and attention to others can force partners into the arms of others, as they feel unloved and ignored. There are also all the other things going on with appearance and lack of libido. No one plans this; it can just happen, all because of the lack of self-control caused by the constant use of the stress button.

We see a rash, a bruise, or a plaster cast, and we sympathise with the sufferer, asking how they did it or whether it hurts. We give them support and cut them some slack. Stress happens behind the eyes, and no one can see it. It is invisible; what people do see, without any context, is an irate, angry, mean individual who does not deserve a chance or explanation. Stress is not recognised, and although it may be distantly acknowledged, it is not given any merit or weight during a challenging situation.

Stress is a life-sucking parasite that becomes part of us. People form opinions of sufferers without knowing them. Some wave it off as a regular everyday occurrence as it takes too much time and effort to understand and help control it. Instead, people become stress monsters who get ignored and pushed out of a friendship, group, team, or workplace.

Trying to avoid stress is pointless, as we must deal with it. If we are not dealing with it, we are thinking about it. Stress is a troublesome daily occurrence for everyone; you do not need to feel alone. Stress needs to be dealt with before we get into serious trouble. The health service is already ready to buckle under the pressure of our ignorance; if stress is something we can start to manage, should we not take it upon ourselves to give it a go? Stage one is recognition. Stress is not a 'norm'. We have no reason why we cannot tackle this modern-day Caveman problem.

THE CAVEMAN PRINCIPLES

We need to wake up, stand up, recognise it and see the damage stress is causing to us and others, then recalibrate our thinking.

Stage two is a simple test. No trick questions; do not overthink it; answer them honestly.

Question	Demands	Yes	No
1	Do you worry about work, performance targets, or deadlines more often than not?		
2	Do you feel that you have too many people relying on you?		
3	Are there conflicts, arguments or challenges between your work and home?		
4	Have you got too much work to do?		
5	Do you work longer hours, staying in the office to catch up?		
	Total		

If you have ticked more than three "Yes" boxes, then I am confident you have too much stress. Digging a little deeper, try another test.

Question	Control	Yes	No
1	Do you take regular breaks at work?		
2	Do you ignore things that are not within your control?		
3	Do you have the confidence to say 'No'?		
4	Have you had a Mammoth free day within the last week?		
5	Have you pressed your button less than three times today?		
	Total		

How many "No's" have you scored? Do I need to point out the obvious? I can hear you say, "Yes, but…" It would be easy for me to type, "It's all in your control." However, I won't because this is your life, and only you can take control of it. The only thing I will say is that there will be no excuses you could give to someone after you realise you have hurt, insulted or mistreated them.

As a retired Police Officer, I know that there are demands that can never be ignored. Let's try one more test. I promise this will be the last one for this chapter anyway.

THE CAVEMAN PRINCIPLES

Question	Lifestyle	Yes	
1	Do you drink alcohol every night?		
2	Do you truly relax on the sofa every night?		
3	Do you feel yourself ranting instead of having a calm conversation?		
4	Do you think that you are overweight?		
5	Do you have a bad diet, eating junk food instead of proper meals, because it is easier?		
	Total		

Add them up; if more than three ticks are in the "Yes" boxes, you have stress, which controls you and your lifestyle.

These three simple checklists are like a stress dipstick. I assume you have put four to five yeses or noes in each question set. By combining the three questionnaires, we can see how stress affects our work, lives, health, and decisions.

Adding 20 more questions to another questionnaire will yield the same results, except you would get bored and frustrated completing them to reach the same conclusion. Now that you know your results, it is up to you to act on them.

Start with a few handy sayings or mantras to use every day. Repeat a few of them in front of a mirror and watch how you react. You will know which one works. Consider using these to start thinking more positively about life.

Life will be too short; I will always want one more day.

Just because I am busy, I may not be productive. Thinking and doing are two very different things. No matter my age, I have an opportunity to live the life that I *can* create.

It all happens for a reason (my personal favourite). Some people I will never get on with; I will expect it and be able to work around them.

An apology is not necessary before I can forgive someone.

There are two days this week that I will never be able to make a difference in my life – yesterday and tomorrow.

We know that we are all stressed. We understand that we are not in control of our buttons. After this acceptance stage, we get to the denial or blame stage. Some will start asking questions.

If all this button is to cause stress, why do we still need it?

If we can now only use the freeze response and cannot use the fight-or-flight actions, surely the button needs to be made redundant.

With the potential harm it can cause, why shouldn't we get it taken out? Take a pill? Or ignore it? Then the Mammoth can jump out whenever it wants, and we won't have to worry about our reaction.

This stage is relatively short-lived once people realise that this is our body and cannot be changed. Millennia of evolution cannot be instantly changed. Things have only really changed for our button and response since the 1980s (ish). Stress is such a significant part of our busy lives that we must remind ourselves that the button has proven to be an excellent and powerful tool in many situations. We still need it, but we should be better trained to manage it.

This next stage starts all the hard work, including understanding the problem and not blaming the button. We need to accept our lack of control over our buttons, but then add understanding and find a method that works for us individually.

We do not want to hand over one of our body's most natural responses to other people, so don't and take control. They are not free to use and abuse our button whenever they want to get a result.

We have relinquished this control, probably because we were taught that we must concentrate on less important things, or we have just followed others when they hand power over to others, learning to do the same.

People do not acknowledge that we live in a materialistic world and that our negative view of society is unhealthy. Considering that most people would be happy doing a responsible job that fits their skills and is paid a reasonable wage, then why do we settle for just a job? No one is ever stuck. We can all retrain. I know of 70-year-olds still working and going back to college and doing a new course, but this is because they want something more, a new challenge, and this change makes them happy because they are doing something about it; there is no perception of being stuck, too old or it is too late. Things happen, and from my experience, I realised that not everything we do is necessarily in our best interests.

I will share what happened and how far I went before I had to examine what was really pushing my button. In this next part, I am not saying that promotion is bad; this was a scenario I had to work through. Promotion may be right for you, but when we chase something so hard, sometimes we can lose focus on what is important.

Many years ago, I wanted a promotion to Sergeant. I sat my exams and became fully qualified. I worked toward building a portfolio of evidence to prove that I could move into the next rank. My focus on promotion caused me to become blinkered, as I had forgotten to enjoy myself and look after others. My drive to reach the next rank alienated me from my friends, colleagues and family. I became a cold, unapproachable individual who did a fantastic job in the eyes of those I thought supported me, my bosses. I willingly handed over my button. They made sure I pressed it to their tune, made me dance to their rhythm, and did not care how many hits of it were made. Nor did I, as I believed there was something to prove. I was worthy of the next rank.

After about four years of chasing promotion and being knocked back constantly, but with the dangling of a carrot, I saw it for what it was.

Continually being told I was good enough to continue in the acting rank but not made substantive, there had to be a problem. I stopped and reassessed what I wanted and what I was trying to achieve. I was exhausted and could not understand why I had not been promoted. I had done everything that was asked of me, but I kept failing my final interviews. The reason was simple: my bosses loved the results I brought in. My interview boards had good write-ups from my immediate boss, but I did not come across as a good manager during my hour-long dialogue because it was not my style. They wanted a puppet to be moulded into something unnatural.

The realisation sent a cold bead of sweat right down my back. I asked myself, "Why am I doing this?" I should have asked myself this question years ago, as it would have saved a lot of upset and a whole load of button presses.

Quickly, I concluded that I was not worried about the extra pay or the respect that the rank brought. I had contemplated this for a while, trying to determine why it was all wrong. I realised I went for it because it was 'expected.' The Police is a ranked institution; it pushes people to climb the promotion ladder.

This hidden expectation had wasted years of my life, caused pain and reputational damage, put friendships on the line and caused unwanted upset in my marriage.

Promotion should be for people who want the extra responsibility of improving other people's lives, not for the betterment of management. There are no excuses for those who abuse another person's button, whether it is a job, family, or personal situation. There needs to be respect.

I can count on one hand the number of good leaders that I'd experienced who supported the challenging work, understood the situation, and guided me. The rest of the managers were awful, dreadful managers, only interested in their results, pushing their teams to breaking point, showing favour to those they liked and unable to manage a diverse team. My drive for promotion disappeared. Even though I had told myself that the extra money could buy me a motorbike or allow me to go on more or better holidays, the dream died, and I never felt better about stepping back.

I shook off the materialist urge that had taken hold of me. To this day, I can recall stepping into my Inspector's office, handing over the stripes, and walking away from promotion for good. I had reassessed what I wanted in my life. If I wanted it to work, I would have to do something different and change who I was. I started to relax, became happy with who I was, and found myself again.

A study by a group of psychologists at the University of Warwick followed 1,000 promoted people. They showed that the higher up in an organisation someone had been able to climb, the worse their mental health became.

They were able to prove that each time someone was promoted, they averaged a gain of an extra 10% of stress, and because of their status as a manager, not wanting to be seen as weak, they also reduced their visits to a doctor by 20%. The psychologists believed this extra pressure came from an increased workload, the growing responsibility they felt, overwork and reduced leisure time.

Professor Oswald (not the one from *Spider-Man*) stated that his team believed that gaining a promotion had no physical benefits; however, they did conclude that it can have a serious impact on someone's mental health.

Many people lose themselves. The more control someone must have in their daily work, the more stress they have. Status is everything; hiding behind a title and ignoring warning signs has only one outcome. When a manager who has forced themselves to change their personality for the role takes control of others, it usually leads to micromanagement. They lose perspective, get frustrated and start demanding more button pushes. Crazier and higher KPIs become the norm, sending the team into a frenzy. Then, when it goes wrong, as it always does, the manager never has to justify every decision or is subjected to scrutiny and checks; the team has increasing stress levels, which is the reason for the failure.

A want for promotion should be a natural process. However, people put themselves through the extra stress, fail as a good manager and then potentially suffer from stress-related illnesses. There is no reflection or realisation before returning to the same role for more punishment, either to themselves or others. People who choose to be promoted are seeking to walk a dangerous path. They are putting more Mammoths in their way, yet only natural leaders in a chosen environment can see a clear route and be able to guide their team through it, yet these individuals are few and far between.

After I decided that a promotion in the police was not suitable for me, I was left with some spare headspace and capacity to help others. This led me to examine human psychology and how it fits into modern-day stress. This decision was the catalyst for creating this book, The Caveman Principles.

Everything Happens for a Reason

Given the damage and impact of stress on modern-day Cavemen, our modern world has a lot to answer for. Unforgiving bosses and unreasonable clients have turned the original cave dweller into a stressed mess, living their lives on the edge of their button, only able to wish that they would not see another mammoth.

Our hectic, stressful lives have created a new belief. That everyone is incompetent. We are no longer working in a close-knit team; many of us are multitasking, working with a constantly changing workforce, and no longer have the stability of a supportive team. Getting the job done is the goal; stepping on toes, shouting, and demanding is the norm; we all know how best to complete any task, and we do not want interference or others' input, even when there is a better way. We do not acknowledge people's personalities or differences; work takes precedence.

I am a "get in there, let's see what we've got" sort of operator. Others prefer to gather as much information as possible, even delaying doing anything positive until they have a plan. Working with these people constantly presses my button. Sometimes, I am physically shaking with the amount of toxins that have been pumped into my system. Busy work diaries and schedules have not given people time to see who we are dealing with. These human interactions have such massive stress implications that they need further explanation.

So, it is good that I have written the next part of this book to explain this issue.

I can go on to give more examples of how our button can be pressed, but it is time for you to recognise your stressful event. Reading is great, but taking action is where the actual results kick in.

Taking command of our button will stop the freeze response and give us back control. Remember, Mammoths are sneaky creatures of habit and can become predictable. Once they have found a good hiding place, they will use it repeatedly. If you have ever grabbed hold of an electric fence, I bet you will do everything to avoid doing it again (unless it is for your YouTube channel), so why can we not bypass the Mammoth's same hiding place?

Insanity is doing the same thing repeatedly and expecting a different result. It will take time as we are all different, and we all have our own unique lives. We as individuals must start looking for the Mammoth's hideouts. Learn to avoid them or better prepare yourself. Finding a new route through the Mammoth minefield will take dedication and effort. Use a diary and describe the stressful events you encounter each day. Boil down the problem, identify button triggers, and you will start to see the same thing come up.

Whether it is the same person, the same client, the same contractor or the same unreasonable demand, there will be a common element. Keep exploring, asking why they are making me feel like this, why do I react, why am I not letting go?

Don't focus on just work; do the same for your home life. Is it the same neighbour, the same argument or the family that demands your time? Keep asking why it bothers you, why you react, and why you can't respond more reasonably.

Learn, recognise, and approach things from a different direction. Try new ways of communicating or start accepting things for what they are. If it is out of your control, why worry? Focus on responding to the situation rather than the person. Do what you can to prepare yourself, plan, take time, and be honest and open about the problem. Tell people you don't know and do not have time, and take the pressure off. Thank people more and be accepting of people's shortfalls.

Looking for the typical hiding spots of the Mammoth, we start to do something positive, preparing ourselves for a better response. This alone will stop the freeze reaction from happening. The more Mammoths we avoid, the more control we gain over our response and button. Once we have mastered this step, we become happier and better people. Not all Mammoths can be avoided, but when we dramatically reduce our exposure to them, these are easier to manage. The more we practice our Mammoth avoidance skills, the more we recognise the initial feelings of when the fight or flight button wants to be pressed.

By reducing our exposure to Mammoths, we regain our strength, which we can use to reduce the demand for more pushes. It is a skill; like all skills, the more practice we have, the better we will become. Hopefully, you can now start to avoid these hairy beasts. Parts 2 and 3 will give you the knowledge and skills to take real action and control the outbursts and button pushes. Before we leave Part 1, here are a few helpful notes and something for you to ponder over.

Individual Cavemen are very different; what works for one may not work for another. Some cavemen can develop a sense of humour and laugh at their mammoths. Comedians make a living of describing their chaotic lives. Being able to do this takes an amazing amount of power back. Other Cavemen can prepare for an attack, can guess where a Mammoth might be hiding and can appear to toughen up or have the ability to go numb. When a Mammoth pounces, they don't freeze; they stare it down and do not react. Other Cavemen have made peace with their Mammoths, saying that not all are bad. These are also known as the 'Zen' Mammoth masters.

People make honest mistakes, but when we are busy, we focus on the wrong things, especially when there is pressure. Modern-day Cavemen cannot control everything, and sometimes, we need to accept things, pick up the pieces, and move on.
When we get a poorly worded email, miss a turn while driving, or get into the wrong queue, we should look for something other than the Mammoth attack. Instead, we should smile and make a choice. There will always be rude and impatient bullies, but when we think about it, they are the minority. These selfish individuals should not be allowed to spoil our outlook on life through their actions. Modern-day Cavemen need to relax more and not expect the worst from everyone.

Cavemen must start thinking more positively and communicating more optimistically. Stop using negative words and see what happens. Try 'and' instead of 'but'; 'but' stops a dialogue. 'And' allows more than one truth, even if they are at odds with each other, 'and' shows willingness and acknowledgement of different potential options.

Both words give the same outcome and deliver a similar message. However, there is no sting in using an 'and'. Also, try to avoid the use of 'don't' as a Caveman's brain does not easily recognise it.

Adults usually start hearing conversations from the second or third word, so starting with "Don't" has already been missed. We must play catch-up to understand what is being said, and we can get frustrated. This might explain why, when a child hears, "Don't drop that," or "Don't put that doughnut down the back of the sofa," they do it. Knowing this information now, we only have ourselves to blame. Always start a conversation with a person's name; people respond quicker. When giving instructions, make it positive. Ask them what you want them to do rather than what you don't.

THE CAVEMAN PRINCIPLES

Life has only one outcome, so make it a worthwhile and happy experience. Like attracts like, so if a Caveman creates a small pocket of trust and a forgiving attitude, others will want to be part of that group. A caveman's life can become easier as we turn negative, nasty environments into happy, relaxed, and productive ones.

Stress is about losing our grip and control. When we have no control over the number of Mammoths we meet daily, we do not control how we deal with them or how we use our buttons.

We must recognise a Mammoth. This is important as they work against and rub us the wrong way. They can ruin lives if we let them.

Get ready for Part Two by stopping thinking the worst of people. Be more positive and more accepting of their mistakes. Change the way that we interact with 'stupid' people. We always have a choice, but it is up to you if you want to make a real difference.

Part Two of this book is coming up. It will continue to help you manage your stress by helping you understand the people in your tribe. Understanding and managing others truly helps to reduce stress.

If that is not enough, the final section, Part Three, will help you make a positive change, as no one seems to be able to make change happen and gets stressed for failing.

Your new knowledge of stress is all you will ever need to get through life. Well done for completing part one. If you are impressed with this book, wait until you have finished the rest of it.

THE CAVEMAN PRINCIPLES

PEOPLE WHO THINK THEY KNOW
EVERYTHING ARE A
GREAT ANNOYANCE TO
THOSE OF US WHO DO.

ISAAC ASIMOV

PART TWO

THE CAVEMAN PRINCIPLES

5.
PEOPLE PROFILING

We do fit into a box.

Personality profiling is not about how someone looks sideways. Profiling is when an individual can identify a unique personal trait within another. Identifying, understanding and then using this knowledge can reduce conflict and help win arguments. The key to successfully profiling another person is the ability to listen. Hearing all the words, not just picking the flavour of the conversation, watching body movements, and going with your instincts will be worth all the effort.

We have all been told we are part of a new and exciting way to do things, rolled out by a manager or someone standing in front of a crowd telling everyone to do this one specific thing to make our life easier. Everyone loves the concept except us, knowing it will never work. In this book section, I will explain why we are all so different, react differently, and deserve to be treated as individuals.

Remember, there will never be a one size that fits all, but there might be a one size that fits a particular character trait.

This section of the book is where we can have a lot of fun. No one was born an expert; we all start with nothing and grow our skills. There is no right or wrong way to profile someone. We do not need to be frightened; give it a go, and when we get it right, it will make a real difference in our daily lives.

Understanding a dark art will start to unravel why some people can be a real help and good company, whilst others we debate if a hitman could visit them. We may not fit into one exact role; very few are pure personalities. There may be elements from all the tribe members you may relate to, but one will shine slightly brighter. This shining persona will be your most decisive role. Also, it is accepted that people 'do' change. Age, experience, and even trauma can change someone's personality, so make sure you read the person in front of you, not the person you thought you knew years before. There is also strong evidence to suggest that you can have a persona at work and a different one at home. This is probably why people turn out to be an all-right bloke when you get your terrible boss into the pub.

Profiling people is a skill; like any skill, practice is key. It will make you a better judge of character. I use personality profiling in all my jobs, but when I was a cop, this skill was often a lifesaver. The ability to quickly work out how a person thinks and operates and know how they will respond can be a massive advantage in any line of work.

Profiling is an essential tool without any credit in today's digital world. Most of us have no time, and we take people at face value. We are too busy to spend a few extra seconds digging a little deeper, not seeing the point of why working someone out is beneficial. Ignoring these skills, we allow genuine opportunities and potential lifelong friends to pass through our busy lives.

Have you ever met someone new and instantly hit it off with them? Do you want to exchange details, swap phone numbers, and even invite them for a drink and a social? There was 'something' there that made us want to spend more time getting to know them; we do not question what that 'something' ever is.

On a different occasion, the 'others' appear. They are the ones we want to punch in the throat within two seconds of meeting them so that we don't have to listen to them anymore. We cannot get away from them quick enough. Afterwards, we do not think about why this is, and we move on.

Chance encounters can be easy to dismiss, especially those in our personal lives. However, in a work environment, we can miss important information on how to deal with these exchanges. It is a good job that I added this part, as I know how stressful it can be to manage these conversations. We will never like everyone, and the ones we don't will push our buttons within seconds: some people we can ignore, but others we will have to work with.

If you could learn how to read someone, name their personality, and understand their mannerisms, would that help? You could learn how to interact with them, know how they think, communicate, and even get them to do what you want; would that make life easier? Managing them and even getting them to your way of thinking; let's be honest, all this would help reduce your daily stress.

If done correctly, you will need to become a people watcher, and it will stop you from jumping to conclusions, making you a formidable person.

Some people seem to have the same reactions and thought processes as others; these can be termed personality traits. Whether they are outward, quiet, or plain crazy, even the ones we despise, they all have a typical feel or the same traits.

When your stress Mammoth appears when dealing with certain types of people, have you stopped to think about who you are dealing with and if there is an easier way?

Profiling has been around for hundreds and even thousands of years. Typically carried out by psychoanalysts and doctors, most theories are highbrow stuff, with valuable and insightful conclusions, but no one has the time to interpret their findings into everyday use. No one outside the profession reads their theories because you need a truck to get the manuscript home and another to carry some medical dictionary to interpret them.

Well, it is a good job I wrote this part of the book, as it is so easy to use when you cut through all the jargon and lingo; this type of life skill should be taught in schools.

To use profiling daily, we have four types of people who come together to make an entire tribe. As a taster, I want to start introducing our team so that you can see who to deal with. The most extreme personalities are the 'Gatherers', who will like reading this book cover to cover. The following few pages will be the juicy stuff for them, giving content and far too much information.

Our 'Hunters' who need information fast to conclude will want to jump ahead a few pages. Just give them the detail they need, or it will send them around the twist. The other two, 'Protectors' and 'Healers', sit in the middle.

I did a lot of research for this book, so if you are interested, please read on; otherwise, skip the next few pages. About 2,000 years ago, there lived a man named Hippocrates.

He was a famous Greek physician who liked putting people into his boxes. He described people as having one of his four humours, linking them to one of the four elements.

- Sanguine traits were linked to Air. These people are lively, social, carefree, talkative and pleasure seekers (Hunters).
- Choleric traits are linked to Fire. These are excitable, impulsive, and restless people with an aggressive side (Protectors).
- Melancholic traits are more Earthy. These people are serious, cautious and of the suspicious type (Gatherers).
- Phlegmatic traits are linked to Water. These individuals are more thoughtful, private, calm, and reasonable (Healers).

Since Hippocrates was one of the first to publish his thoughts, very little has changed. The same reasoning with only new words and a slightly different take might seem new, but the essence has always remained the same.

Most new theories have come since the early 1900s, with a resurgence at the beginning of the second millennium.

There are a few more noteworthy people. Carl Gustav Jung, a well-known Swiss psychiatrist and psychotherapist from the 1920s, whose name is etched within every psychology student's head, put his twist on Hippocrates' theories. He published his book on psychological types, describing four noted functions. His personalities experienced the world through sensation, intuition, feeling, and thinking. Then, he divided them into more boxes based on whether they were introverted or extroverted, rational (judgmental) or irrational (perceiving). So, in theory, he made each of the four traits either friendly or shy; this was his contribution.

1928, William Moulton Marston created his troop, which was used in the DISC assessment. It is still trending, with some companies using it for recruiting, believing they will find the right candidate. He was some boring-brained theory boffin; however, to his credit, he also created the well-known superhero Wonder Woman.

For a white-coated geek, he created and dressed a female superhero in one of the most iconic uniforms, which has stood the test of time. Also, this geek designed and built the first Polygraph machine (the lie detector). His DISC theory allowed people an inward view of themselves and how they faced daily situations.

- Dominance – More powerful with an unfavourable environment outlook.
- Inducement – More powerful with a favourable environment outlook.
- Submission – Less powerful with a favourable environment outlook.
- Compliance – Less powerful with an unfavourable environment outlook.

See, I told you that you might need a dictionary or thesaurus and some time to decipher things.

A mother-and-daughter team—I believe they were a pair of Gatherers—created one of the best-known theories for defining people's personalities. The Myers-Briggs Type Indicator (MBTI) was created in 1962, using Carl Jung's original theories and combining them with their take on things. They created 16 personality types, but they were still based on a four-person style principle.

For me, this was far too complicated and too many to choose from.

Another person worth mentioning is David Keirsey. His work on the subject is one of my favourites. In his 1978 book, he showed how to work people out using his Keirsey Temperament Sorter. He pushed people into;
- Artisans
- Guardians
- Idealists
- Rationals

Finally, the last person who gave colours to people's personality traits was a process accredited to Don Lowry. He did this in 1979, using Gold, Orange, Green and Blue to describe the same four traits.

If different authors have shoved the same four types of people into the same boxes within the last 2,000 years, then having just one more that is simple and written for those of us without a doctorate to be able to use every day isn't going to make a huge difference.

As a cop, I found the use of profiling incredibly helpful. My job taught me that no one is 100% truthful; people feel they need to protect themselves, either wanting to hold the truth back or changing the narrative.

By identifying the four traits and exploiting an understanding of how victims and suspects operate, I gained a valuable advantage, which worked perfectly for me. The aim was to gain trust and manage interviews, and with this incredible ability, I could draw out the truth whilst maintaining a rapport. I got some spectacular results: suspects admitting offences they tried their hardest to hide, even shaking my hand afterwards because they felt the pressure release, victims being able to open up, covering sensitive aspects that enabled me to grab a much-needed break in the case, all thanks to other people's theories.

Working years in interviewing people, I changed, modified, updated and created something that worked for me. It is time to share this process and share my profiling thoughts with others. But I am going to do it in the Caveman style.

6.

USING THE CTS FOR THE PEOPLE IN 'OUR TRIBE'

We all have a role to play in our tribe.

Hunters can rejoin us here, and now that we are back together again, it is time for a bit more fun. This is where we become crowd-watching psychoanalysis experts.

Before we get into it, the most critical point is that People change! Regardless of how they work, they will become different people at home. When people are ill, stressed or out of their comfort zone, their personalities will change, and when alcohol or even drugs are involved, do not expect the same personality to be present. My advice is that if you want to manage people, you should focus on how they present at the moment they are being observed, and not on a survey or online test they did 2 years ago.

The CTS (Caveman Tribe Sorter) is straightforward. Anyone who uses it can identify another's personality traits. From these traits, we pop them into our tribe. These placements can change, be amended, and even flip-flop between characters. The important thing is to give it a go; no one will know what you are doing unless you are holding this book in front of them whilst doing it. If you get it wrong, try another. Practice makes perfect. It took about 12 years for me to get good at identifying people, but I did not have this book to help.

Identifying people through the CTS for their roles in our tribes should be fun. The characters are Hunters, Protectors, Gatherers, or Healers, all needed to produce an active, healthy group of people. Once someone has a character, try the tips for communicating with them to improve relationships and, more importantly, reduce your stress.

What if you get it wrong? There is no room for 'what ifs', so give it a go. Never be afraid of trying something new; you might surprise yourself.

Start with friends and family, pop them into a role and see what happens. If you think you got it wrong, change it and try again; when you get it right, you will feel the connection and grow in confidence.

Self-perception can easily get distorted, so you should rely on something other than doing a self-assessment. If you ask someone what they think of themselves, their reply may differ from what society thinks.

An example is to be a passenger in a car, ask the driver if they think they are good at driving, and then watch their response. They should start driving more carefully and be more considerate. Everyone believes they are the best driver; however, when someone challenges this thought, it instantly changes their perception. Our self-perception tells us we are great drivers, and no one can criticise us. I often saw this when dealing with motoring offences in my old job. The average rational person becomes defensive and difficult. It was never the ticket that the offending motorist disliked, it was what it represented: a criticism of their driving. Using personality profiling always helped diffuse the situation, but many of my colleagues just left motorists angry and frustrated.

The same happens when people are asked about any character trait. They respond in a way they feel is right, putting themselves in a more favourable light. Very few people are honest with themselves, so it is always good to get a second opinion.

Self-perception is one thing; another is Nature versus Nurture. This is where a person's true personality can be masked, covered up by an expectation placed on them by family, jobs, responsibilities and even an education. Trying to characterise someone with a military background can be tricky; they may present themselves as one type after years of harsh exposure, but they are entirely different; underneath all that bravado could be someone sensitive and indecisive.

They might have even squashed themselves into a role through expectation, thinking that is where they belong. When the years of drill and discipline, with the expectation of everyone to be the same, are finally wiped away, their true personality trait should start to emerge.

Most of all, make it fun. Share the CTS with others and get them involved; profiling people becomes more manageable when others do it with you, sharing ideas and results.

THE CAVEMAN PRINCIPLES

Let's start by asking the first set of questions to help categorise them into their tribes.

Question	CTS Part 1 – Open or Closed?	Yes	No
1	Do they talk about themselves a lot?		
2	Do they have opinions that they want to share?		
3	Are they approachable?		
4	Can you tell what they are thinking?		
5	Can you interpret their reactions?		
6	Are they likely to honestly respond to a personal question?		
7	Do you trust your judgement of them, just at face value?		
	Total		

There are no tricky questions; it's a simple yes or no response. Add up the totals, showing who is open and who is closed. If the " Yes " number of ticks outnumber the "No" number, that person is open; if the opposite, they are closed.

Open people are usually approachable and have easy-going personalities, and people tend to know a lot about them. Being closed is the exact opposite. Closed individuals are the ones people cannot read; new people are wary around them, and most will want to give them a wide berth.

Next, are they Direct or Indirect with people?

Question	CTS Part 2 – Direct or Indirect?	Yes	No
1	Do they say what they mean?		
2	Do they get straight to the point of any conversation?		
3	Do you get a closed reply when you ask an open question (a yes or no answer)?		
4	Do they tell people what they need?		
5	Are they blunt, an ability to say 'no' without giving any explanation?		
6	Do they usually go with the truth even if it hurts someone's feelings?		
7	Do they take conversations too literally, without looking for any hidden meanings?		
	Total		

This one can be a little more difficult. The trick to answering these questions is to avoid dissecting them. Please keep it simple; it is either a yes or a no. Be brutal if you must.

If there are more "Yes's" than "No's," then the person is a direct communicator, and if there are more "No's," then they are indirect communicators.

A Direct communicator does not mince words; they appear not to care what people think of them when they speak their minds. If they have something to say, they will say it. If they have to give instructions, there will be no messing. They will not want to hear arguments or tolerate anyone asking 'why?' They tell people 'How it is'.

Indirect people are less forceful and more tactful. They are concerned about other people's perceptions and emotions. They are uncomfortable giving instructions without explanation and do not like saying things that would upset others. They would instead take a side than provide an opinion. The extreme of these types of people will never be able to fire anyone.

Telling if a person is Open or Closed, Direct or Indirect, allows us to put them into our CTS and give them a role within the tribe.

Open & Direct People are Hunters.

Closed & Direct People are Protectors

Closed and Indirect People are Gatherers.

Open and Indirect People are Healers.

THE CAVEMAN PRINCIPLES

7.
HUNTERS

It will all work out in the end.

Hunters are the Open and Direct tribe members. Of the four basic elements, they are the closest to Air. Looking back at our ancestral Caveman tribe, we would see the Hunter telling everyone how important they are, that they are the gel that holds the tribe together. These Cavemen were the main Hunters of the group, hence the name. They would have been fearless, going out of the cave to hunt for dangerous animals so that the tribe could survive and, more importantly, to get praise for doing it. They were willing to put their lives on the line and, in return, the expected respect. They were the wannabe celebrities of their time, striving for more attention. They would need fanfare as they left for a hunt and an even bigger hero's welcome when they returned.

There is no doubt that Hunters, living so dangerously, would have been the jokers of the tribe. When not out hunting, they would get bored quickly and need entertainment.

They would have thought it funny to have pushed a sabre-toothed tiger into a cave where their mother-in-law sat to laugh at what happened.

It was just a bit of harmless fun, hilarious listening to her screaming and banging around as she chased it out of the cave. When the Hunters got caught and chastised for doing this, defending their actions would be easy; it was just a bit of fun, as they would not understand empathy at that moment. They'd need time to reflect on their actions before being more reasonable.

Hunters are the lively ones of any group, but they are focused when they have an important task, such as hunting. Adaptive, agile, and always willing to test their boundaries. They live by their results, getting upset if someone is not pulling their weight. If they missed their prey, it would be someone else's fault, and whoever is to blame must hide. Quick thinkers, being able

to think on their feet, ready to react, constantly monitoring and reassessing situations. The more dangerous the situation, the better they work. They did not hunt with rules. Things change momentarily, and they need their decisions to be more fluid, like the air.

Whilst they hunted Mammoths, they knew there were too many variables and a set of rules would always need to be more flexible; they preferred to work things out as they went along, and if someone got hurt, that happens.

Back to the present day, apart from a few extra feet in height and less body hair (although sometimes I am not so sure; there have been a few gorillas in the showers at the gym, but never mind), not much has changed for the modern-day Caveman. Today's Hunters are still a massive part of our tribe. Although they may not be out hunting for mammoths, they will have found an important job for which they want the same recognition.

Hunters are inquisitive and enthusiastic about anything new and exciting. They are carefree and open and can talk to anyone about anything. They make great connections.

Still showing they have no fear, throwing caution to the wind, this is untrue. Deep down, they are incredibly rational about their fear, and they have a sense of the presence of danger. Hunters perceive danger differently and uniquely to everyone else; they are more accustomed to Mammoth attacks and have a higher threshold of what being "dangerous" means. Most daredevils will be Hunters, as will most extreme sports enthusiasts. They rationalise and assess situations astonishingly quickly. This is why they are the first to accept a challenge; they are confident because they consider their abilities, and the task asked is equally matched.

Hunters need fun and are always looking for new opportunities. Whether it is a new hobby or skill, they throw themselves into a new obsession until they appear bored and find another one. A Hunter needs to have a hobby that delivers a quick win. They start enthusiastically, learning enough before justifying whether they need to continue. If the hobby requires years of training, it will find its way to the back of a garage, along with the rest of the other hobbies, sporting equipment and strange incomplete projects, ready to be brought back out when there is a clear-out.

Hunters need constant stimulation, even being tempted to poke a wasp nest (physically and metaphorically). If they think it will entertain them, they will do it. Hunters appear to have no boundaries and no problem playing practical jokes on strangers, seniors, and loved ones. They want people to laugh at their pranks, see it as a service, and expect praise for raising morale.

Hunters are seen as 'loose cannons' rolling around a ship's deck, wreaking havoc and destruction on anything getting in their way. They live for the 'moment' and are always in the 'here and now'. Seen as not serious, they appear not to be planning for anything, but they are formidable when needing to move at pace if there is no plan.

They look forward to the future and are not interested in the past. This will infuriate others, as Hunters want to keep moving forward and only want to debrief something or add a lesson learnt exercise if they benefit from it. Otherwise, it is seen as highlighting mistakes, which they will find embarrassing. Hunters learn quickly from mistakes; they constantly self-reflect, making mental notes and not dwelling on them. They are not interested in going over it again to appear to learn something. The learning was already done. They have a 'now let's move on' attitude.

Hunters use their gut feelings, applying them regularly. They quickly make difficult decisions, which can seem cold and unemotional. Hunters can be surprisingly logical, their hearts always in the right place, but this can be overridden instantly with a gut reaction if it is strong enough. They cannot explain why they make every choice; they know it's right.

All Hunters will push their family into the world, getting their children to stand on their own two feet as quickly as possible. They want them to succeed and will struggle to keep supporting them. Hunters are those people who go on world trekking holidays with their 5-year-old child.

A Hunter wants to inspire passion and create independence in people. They want them to be self-reliant, stand up for themselves, and be the best they can be, and not need constant attention and support. Hunters need their own time and have little interest in giving ongoing support. If someone becomes too needy, a Hunter will become frustrated.

In business, Hunters are incredible negotiators and brilliant stakeholder managers. They have a unique ability to talk to anyone, using humour and being able to read the situation. Their open personality and direct approach make meetings fun and productive. If a Hunter sees an opportunity to better themselves, they will jump in with both feet, even before knowing the outcome of where the training may lead. They might not ride the opportunity train to the end because if they see another, better one, they will switch, even if it means going in a different direction. They are, however, guaranteed to keep spectators frustrated, entertained, and enthralled throughout the journey. Hunters are incredibly persuasive and can convince people with tales of experience, some confidence and a limited knowledge, no matter how deep it is, they will convey their idea without fault.

Hunters are performers, not spectators. They have pride and want to win because losing is embarrassing. They have no problem embellishing a few facts to make sure they are on the winning side of an argument.

Detail could be a more substantial point; Hunters hate it. They only need brief instructions and want to work the rest out for themselves. Hunters are 'learn as they go' and do not rely on or want to be part of a 'recognised' learning process. To a Hunter, Ikea furniture instructions are a waste of paper.

Once a Hunter thinks they have mastered a skill, they instantly want to teach it to others. They want to demonstrate this expertise and start conversations to show off this new understanding. Hunters can assimilate information quickly; giving them access to the internet and challenging them is the best way to utilise this ability.

Hunters love being seen as authorities; they can spend hours finding new techniques, stories, or practices. Hunters have a short attention span; if they do not see results quickly and do not get the recognition they want, they will find something new that they will put their effort into. They will never read long, essential emails and ignore user manuals. They know how to pull the information they need just by looking at the text, regardless of any risk of not reading all of it. If you want them to get a message, put it in the first paragraph. Otherwise, it will get ignored and then deleted.

Not knowing detail will always get a Hunter into trouble, but they more than make up for it in their ability to adapt and learn fast. The rules for sending emails to a Hunter are as follows: make it short. Refrain from explaining why you are sending it; get to the point, and use bullet points and bold text to highlight the important stuff.

Hunters learn much faster when performing a task. They prefer to be walked through a set of instructions rather than having to read things step-by-step. They are 'kinaesthetic' learners.

Getting something wrong is difficult for a Hunter; even with undisputable evidence, they will try to ignore it. They will start justifying, adding their reasoning to lessen the blame. The fact that they are wrong will not change their opinion or thought process. Even if they admit otherwise, internally, they will think they are right; they want to move on and stop any further embarrassment.

Hunters find it hard to apologise for mistakes. Instead, they prefer to make grand gestures and show they can change in other ways rather than say sorry.

All Hunters are fighters fighting to keep their position in the tribe. With their morals and beliefs, they have no concerns about telling someone what they think and why they believe it is the case.

Without variety, problems arise, especially when a Hunter gets bored. They will dismiss the importance of a task if it becomes mundane. They dislike people who do not 'get' it; they stay with the same type of friends, all of whom understand a Hunter and show signs of cherishing the friendship (buying the next round). Hunters are generous but do not want to justify their actions if they decide not to indulge others. They have a thousand thoughts going around their heads and choose their audience; they will ignore people they think are picky and want to lecture them about life; life is too short for that.

Hunters can be considered misleading, saying one thing and doing another. This tends to happen while a Hunter is still working things out. When asked for their thoughts, they will blurt out their current thinking without working things through. Hunters are like the air; they are fluid and can change their minds quickly if they believe they will get a better outcome.

The glass is always half full, with Hunters keen to start things, even if the plan is only partly developed. Any changes made, there is a reasoning; even if they appear flawed, they make perfect sense to a Hunter as they work things out. No amount of complaining will get a Hunter to admit they made the wrong decision. Their quick thinking and decision-making skills will keep everything intact. Even if it doesn't, a Hunter will still come out of it smelling of roses.

Use a short PowerPoint presentation if you want a Hunter to become productive, especially in a meeting. If you must, add pictures and use fewer words or none if you can.

Hunters could do better with e-learning packages; they follow the same principles as PowerPoints. If forced to complete them, they find a way to get to the end as quickly as possible, with no learning involved. They will probably even brag about the speed of getting to the end, never learning the objective. They take potshots at multiple-guess questions and retake them repeatedly without additional input to get a 'pass'.

Hunters adore quick wins and easy tasks. They are happy to complete 20 short tasks in a day rather than one massive task over a week, but now and then, they want to be challenged, so be prepared to throw them a curveball.

If a Hunter loses focus, a gentle reminder of their original task puts them back on track. Giving praise is the easiest way to get a Hunter to restart work. Make them feel that they are the only person for this task, that only they are trusted to complete it to the expected high standard they are capable of. This will reignite them.

If you want to upset a Hunter and get them to push their button, restrict them. Stopping them from doing what they want to do, especially how they want to do it, will lead to conflict. They hate micro-management; it is a form of attack, and they will fight ferociously, even wrestle dirty, to get what they want, when they want, and how they want it.

Hunters need to be kept busy, but only with essential tasks. Even if it is the most mundane task in the world, it must be sold as the 'key' to the whole process; it is the most important job that needs to be done, and they have been chosen to do it.

Expecting them to do 'nothing' is inviting trouble. Don't hold them back if work is waiting to be done and a Hunter wants to get on with it. They can find ways to entertain themselves; they will overstep their mandate and interfere with other people's work, even if they have no clue what that other person is doing. However, they will work relentlessly to do their bit if they believe they can plug a gap.

Hunters handle short, stressful situations exceptionally well; they stay calm and unflustered because of their quick reasoning. If a Hunter is placed in a long-term stressful situation, they will lose their cool and get angry because their ongoing effort does not yield a result. If there is no end to a stressful situation, they will probably explode, so expect carnage.

Hunters bottle up stress like other tribe members, but when they reach saturation point, they do not give any notice before they fly off the handle. They appear to cope right up to the point that they bite someone's head clean off. Then, it gets a bit messy, especially if it is the boss. Once a Hunter has vented their frustration, they instantly forget about it and expect others to do the same.

They pick up where they left off, carrying on as if nothing happened.

Hunters want to be everyone's friend. They treat all others the same, not necessarily as their equal. They have no presumptions until they know differently. Hunters do not recognise people's personal boundaries and have no problem being 'overly friendly' even if they have just met. They think it is acceptable to call their doctor by their first name and think of their big boss as a 'mate'.

However, a Hunter quickly learns where someone's line is. Telling a Hunter what is comfortable and what isn't will change their response, but don't make a scene out of it. They will conform if they are not belittled; if people snap at them, it becomes a game. They will continue to overstep the mark until they get bored or there is a huge argument.

Hunters are typically trusting, seeing the good in people until they experience a few harsh facts about them. Hunters do not participate in grudge matches; they can ignore people they no longer want to interact with and not feel bad about it.

They have long memories; if people cross a Hunter, they can expect it to be actioned years later. This may seem childish, but there is nothing anyone can do to change the decision. Only when the person apologises and makes it up to the Hunter will things be brushed aside, even if it gets uncomfortable for other people.

Keeping Hunters productive and utilising their natural abilities is easy. Setting them goals and playing into their ego helps. Tell them they were the first to come to mind if you want to create an impact. Do not set firm deadlines; never detail how it should be done unless asked. Telling them that it is a real challenge will whet their appetite.

If you want them to take on more work, they need to be appreciated for their effort when the task's result is offered, even if it differs from your expected standard. Whatever they show as their finished product, even if it is not what was expected, heap on praise and recognition before you ask them to change or modify any of it.

Hunters do not like to be wrong and hate to be criticised, so bear that in mind. If you need to speak to a Hunter about the quality of their work, do not do this in an office full of people; it will maximise the embarrassment. Instead, take them for a coffee and relax them. Avoid giving feedback in a formal setting, such as across a desk. Hunters react better when they see the whole person, as they pick up on body language more than any other tribe member. Telling a Hunter that they got it wrong over the phone or by email will not result in a positive outcome.

Hunters are proud; they want to show their achievements to everyone. Awards and praise are a huge motivator. If you upset a Hunter and are pushed over the edge, you will know about it quickly. When a Hunter feels threatened, they activate their button very quickly. They will be ferocious, fighting and arguing until they win or suffer burnout.

If there is a need to give feedback, start by talking about positive achievements and then slip in a comment. Lead them to the issue and ask them why it went wrong; it will get a better response than pointing it out. Surprisingly, Hunters are good reflectors, so they have probably already gone through their process and have worked out what they would do differently next time.

They generally do not need to discuss these things in depth, so don't drag it out once they have spoken about it. Finish by adding a phrase to make them feel better, something along the lines that they are still trusted and are recognised for their hard work.

A formal meeting should be considered only if a Hunter needs to be disciplined; otherwise, keep it light and friendly. You will get much more out of this type of discussion.

Tips for Hunters when they deal with the other tribal members.

HUNTER VS HUNTER

When a Hunter meets with another Hunter, it will be a match made in heaven, but only for a short while. Both will feed off the other's enthusiasm and ideas. It will be an explosive combination of challenging and enjoying each other's success. They will be great support, coming up and sharing their next crazy idea. An initial strong friendship, even spending much time with each other. Then, they will start to lose interest, and neither will be willing to stroke the other's ego, so one will begin to sabotage the relationship.

THE CAVEMAN PRINCIPLES

They will throw spanners in, no longer available to the other, and the friendship will quickly crash and fizzle out.

Hunters are great together when everything is equal, but if one Hunter appears to be more successful, this is the beginning of the end. All the limelight will be on the stronger Hunter; they will enjoy this attention and expect recognition. This leads to the underdog scenario, where the losing Hunter no longer feels worthy. Fighting for some attention from the other, more successful Hunter will fail quickly, and they will find it easier to look elsewhere.

They will look for someone they can compete with and potentially beat.

The stronger of the two Hunters will continue enjoying being the top dog and expect to continue a friendship until they realise a gap in their circle of friends; hunters do not pick up on subtle hints. They do not immediately see empathy from another's point of view. When dynamics change in a Hunter pairing, it usually spells the end. Hunters do not like to show weakness or speak about not being equal, commonly referred to as 'respect'.

Hunters expect attention but will not ask for it. They are loud and will show off to get eyes on them, but they are one-trick ponies; if it does not work, they try it on someone else.

HUNTER VS PROTECTOR

Hunters and Protectors can be a perfect match or a fight waiting to happen. Hunters see Protectors as being far too serious, and as they have no problem poking the 'hornet's nest', it can go either way. Hunters will not understand why a Protector can suddenly go off on one, as it was 'only a joke'.

Generally, Hunters and Protectors have mutual respect and get along in a team. Both appear to be dedicated and hard-working, which is essential to them both. Neither will beat around the bush when delivering a complex message, but they will deliver it differently.

The Hunter's direct approach will appear softer, and they may add some humour. A Protector will not pull the punch, telling it how it is.

Problems arise when a Hunter believes they have done a good enough job and finds something more enjoyable to do rather than to a standard expected by a more rigid Protector. The Hunter will not be concerned about not finishing a task, justifying their actions and saying that the new task is a better use of their time, even if they had nothing to show. Protectors will not see this as a justification and believe the Hunter to be lazy. Protectors have a set mind of completing one task before moving on, whereas the Hunter is happy to chop and change, do a bit on each until it is finished, or find a better solution.

A Hunter can learn a lot from a Protector, such as becoming more focused and understanding why completing tasks to a high standard is good. The challenge for a Hunter is that a Protector needs them to cut out the crap, so they need to work on ways to communicate more effectively. Explaining their thought process quickly, without going off tangent, will impress a Protector. If a Hunter needs to improve a relationship with a Protector, they need to be more considerate and serious around them. Hunters taking responsibility and ownership of menial tasks without a fight or expecting any form of thanks is a good start.

HUNTER VS GATHERER

A Hunter and a Gatherer pairing is like watching a game of Buckaroo. You know the donkey will kick off, but you are determining at what point. When the donkey finally kicks, it will make everyone jump and give any spectators a cause for a laugh. Hunters are free-air spirits, and Gatherers are earthy, process-driven, fixated individuals. Gatherers do not understand the Hunter's 'suck it and see' outlook. They would instead think about it, come up with a plan, discuss it and then do it just once, not the 'jump in and have a go' scenario that will require a second attempt.

A Hunter believes that a rigid and fixed mindset of a Gatherer does not see the whole picture, but a Gatherer wants to see more than what's on offer, and this is why they seem far too tentative and indecisive to a Hunter. A Gatherer will never see a problem the same way as a Hunter. No other pairing of personality types is as far apart as these. The fluidity and rigid natures of both mean that the other will reject any process they come up with. When a Hunter tries to explain a result to a Gatherer, the Hunter will talk about all the exciting and beautiful results they feel would work the best. A Gatherer does not use emotion; they only want facts and how the results will be quantified. They will want to know that a process was followed, so if it needs to be corrected, it can be observed or changed the next time. Hunters do not understand this inability to be spontaneous, resulting in friction.

Hunters and Gatherers disagree; they both think their way is the best. They start being 'nice,' but there is only one way this will end.

To Hunters, Gatherers continually ask 'stupid' questions rather than just getting on and working out the answer. Both will get more frustrated and annoyed as the relationship continues. Most interactions between this pairing will result in the Hunter shouting and storming off, with the Gatherer withdrawing from the task and refusing to cooperate with the Hunter ever again.

There is very little that can be done for these two. Only when the Buckaroo kicks can the Hunter reset it with an apology.

They will think it is successful until they both start to load the donkey again, and then we all know what happens next.

Hunters who want the best result when working with a Gatherer must learn to bite their tongues and accept that others are in this relationship. For a successful pairing, they should work in different offices. They need to limit contact, both in person and by email. Scheduling short, regular meetings will appease both sides. The aim is to put only a few things on the donkey at any time and not let the donkey kick off.

HUNTER VS HEALER

Hunters and Healers are both very open tribe members. They both enjoy talking and dealing with emotions. They get on particularly well with each other and will find themselves becoming good friends.

Hunters will become comfortable in a friendship with a Healer and become more adventurous, which the Healer will not like but will go along for the sake of their friendship. The direct nature of the Hunter means they become the ideas person, suggesting where to go and when to meet up. The Healer can start withdrawing and feel a bit of a spare part. The Hunter must recognise this, as a Healer will not mention it. Hunters can take over in these relationships, so being mindful will help. If, in the pairing, the Hunter speaks to new people, the Healer will need to be introduced to them all. The Healer will appreciate this and feel more secure in the friendship, knowing they are not being replaced. Healers and Hunters make excellent companions. The Healer's indirect nature means the Hunter's 'over-the-top' behaviour will not be challenged; it will be ignored, to the Hunter's joy. Providing a Hunter checks how a Healer is feeling regularly, which can seem a lot for a Hunter, will mean the world to the Healer and set the friendship on a better balance.

Spending time alone discussing personal or business matters will score highly for the Healer. There is nothing more endearing to a Healer than knowing the person, with some personal stuff, about a Hunter. Deep down, a Healer is in awe of a Hunter, of how carefree they appear. If a Hunter remembers some personal things about a Healer, it shows a Healer some respect.

8.
PROTECTORS

Get on with it.

Protectors have both Closed and Direct personality traits. They are closest to the Fire element and are seen as the scariest of the tribe members. Our Caveman Protector ancestors will have known they had an essential job, probably the chief, but they would not have gone on and on about it.

They would have been big and tough and able to defend the tribe from any outside threats or aggressors. Protectors would have been the conformers, the ones who lived by the tribe's rules, ensuring they were enforced and that people were punished for breaking them.

They will have followed these rules and agreements to the letter, getting angry and upset when people broke them or tried to bend them.

Protectors will have been the disciplinarians of the tribe. Their job of protecting the cave and its occupants will have been their sole purpose, and

THE CAVEMAN PRINCIPLES

every waking day will be dedicated to this task. They will have believed there is no room for fun as they had an important task to complete. They think they are selflessly working for everyone else's benefit. Because they enforced the rules and pushed for punishment, the tribe feared them for their authoritarian outlook, but they did not care as their task was protecting the tribe. They are "not here to make friends at work" kind of people.

If they think someone is purposefully exposing the tribe to unnecessary danger, they will take matters into their own hands to stop it, following the same steps. The Protector will stop the wrong from happening, fix the problem, and then deal with the person causing the problem.

Protectors will have been seen as big and strong, not necessarily physically but certainly mentally. Thorough and logical, they have a compass for right and wrong. They have an overriding drive to look after those who were taken advantage of and needed protection. They defend their tribe, even when it must be protected against stupidity.

Modern-day Protectors will mostly have the same outlook. They probably wear slightly better-fitting clothes and have better dental care, but their feeling of responsibility will remain the same.

Protectors want to be in control and, therefore, in charge. Their common saying is, "If people do as I say, there will be no problem." They may not necessarily want to be the top honcho, but they cannot tolerate someone in a powerful position doing a lousy job. They are the only ones that genuinely understand the hierarchy and will work hard to get a promotion so that they can put right the wrongly appointed "buffoon" from making bad decisions. The drive to do things right pushes them rather than argue with a superior.

Protectors are the most balanced, honest tribe members who love to hand out tasks. However, they are the epitome of the saying, "Do what I say, not what I do", meaning they are great teachers but

terrible students. They are very pushy and incredibly stubborn, especially when they believe they are correct, which will be all the time. They want people to work hard; fun is not allowed until results are delivered, and enjoying things means there will be delays, and it will take people's focus away from a task. People cannot ease off unless they are on top of all their work or if a workday is ending and all objectives have been achieved. Only once the job is complete will a Protector be happy to party, and they party as hard as they work; they are intense, formidable people in and out of work.

Protectors are efficient - matter-of-fact individuals, and they have strong personal values. They believe that people need a strong work ethic and demand that people and institutions take responsibility for their actions. Protectors have fiery tempers and hate it when people cannot understand the importance of following rules. They have little sympathy for the people who break them; they believe individuals should accept all the consequences; if they decide to step outside of the guidelines, then they deserve what comes their way.

Protectors like to be correct. If you ask a Protector, they will tell you they are always right. Protectors are total control freaks. They do not want people messing with rules. If the rules say that people need to follow a process, then people need to follow it; no shortcuts, follow the rules. When someone tries to make life better by shortcutting, and it takes the process outside the rules, a Protector will not like it, and they will not shut up about it, regardless of the outcome.

Being a Protector means that they prefer the task to be completed the right way. If someone wants to mess around with doing it a new way, then it will not produce the same outcome, and a new process is needed. If there is a schedule to follow, the rules mean people must prepare for and then follow the timings; otherwise, it is wrong.

Protectors prefer to be given tasks that have a specific outcome to them. They like to measure results, especially if it comes with a number. These measurements must quantify something, whether cost, effort or a requirement; they love KPIs. Protectors like to complete tasks, show the result, notch up another count and then move on to the next task. They are results-driven, orientated to achieve, and happy to start a new task immediately after finishing the last one. They like to keep a tally and use it to prove their abilities.

A Protector is an effective team organiser; their focus is that everyone must be pulling their weight.

They appear bossy and sometimes need help understanding why others cannot do a simple job, regardless of their skill set or abilities. They can be seen as patronising, uncaring and even aggressive when others fail. A task can consume a Protector and make them unaware of their dwindling communication skills as they focus on efficiency rather than being polite. Protectors can switch between conversations very quickly and can become upset when others cannot keep the thread of the conversation because, as far as they are concerned, that topic has been addressed.

Protectors can come across as know-it-alls. They spend hours learning how to do a job properly and can quickly become an authority on the subject. They are incredibly reliable and will not mince their words. If they need to tell someone 'How it is,' then they will.

Protectors are among the more responsible people in the tribe. They have an air of authority, and with that fiery temper, if people try to cross them, they are either brave or stupid. Give them a task and allow them to get on with it; they will follow the rules and bring back a result fast.

Protectors believe in common sense, but not if it breaks the rules. They are conventional in sticking to traditions, acceptable behaviours, and skills. They preach these ways of working to all those who do not conform. Protectors can be pretty intense in their 'negotiations' and 'suggestions', but they do not like arguing. They choose logic over emotion.

Protectors are the first to challenge any poor behaviour, going straight to the source, not the gossip network. They have high standards, and they do not like people who are tardy or unprofessional. They are outspoken about these things and have no concerns about telling individuals that they have let the side down. Embarrassing people in front of others is not a concern. They want people to do what is expected of them, no ifs, no buts.

If a Protector has a good manager, they will settle into their role and are guaranteed to be brilliant workers.

If they believe their boss is weak or not doing a good job, their focus changes, and they will want to be in charge. If they think they can do a better job, they set their sights on working their way up the ladder through hard work and dedication.

Protectors do not like asking just anyone for help. When given an unfamiliar task, they will learn a role by seeking people they trust and who are authority figures on the subject. They will master a new skill and produce quality results. Although they can complete numerous tasks simultaneously, they do not like to sign off on a task until they believe everything has been done, which means a thorough check. A massive list of things to do does not bother a Protector, as there is order and a process.

Protectors are the moral moderators when people step out of line. They try to mould people into how they think others should react, wanting "mini-me's" because this means people are doing what they are expected to do.

Protectors are so task-oriented that they prefer to save time. If a conversation is needed, they make sure the point is made quickly, and only when there is time will there be some small talk. A quick hello is usually their limit, and this can even be dispensed with. They want answers, and they want them now, especially when they want to finish a task.

Protectors have such a strong sense of duty and belonging that they find it difficult to ignore anything; it does not feel right. They want to be respected for what they can achieve and to get some form of recognition for the work they have done. They are not concerned about big announcements; a personal "thanks" will do.

Credit must be given to a Protector for their genuine hard work and effort. They will feel devalued if they detect any funny business, sarcasm, or misgivings in the praise. Protectors will tackle the next challenge with or without a thanks. However, if praise is not given when necessary, they have no problem asking for feedback to force out any gratitude.

Most Protectors seek security and trust in authority. Even if they know that those above them may be incompetent, they know their place. They are loyal and steadfast to managerial decisions; they believe in hierarchy, rank, file, and order.

They understand that management structures are there for a reason and do not believe in undermining them. They also want others to respect them, especially if a Protector is above them.

Protectors are loyal to their work, their family, and their friends. They will defend these institutions and not stand for anyone disrespecting people they know.

Protectors are very adept at understanding and implementing rules. With those they trust, they know which rules must be adhered to and where people may be allowed to stretch them. Protectors are pretty practical and understand that no 'one rule' fits all. They will enable some bending if the result turns out the same, but they will resort to the black-and-white of doing it properly if they don't. If they need to, they will step outside the rules, provided it is ethical and in the spirit of achieving the goal, but this is not their comfortable place.

Protectors like information, but not details. They want things to be spelt out, a good bullet point view, and short, simple, detailed reports. Protectors pick up other viewpoints very quickly; they like people to be accurate, factual and brief so it can save time.

Protectors are quick visual learners; they watch and replicate what they see. They are fast learners, and if the pace of teaching is too slow, their button gets pushed, and they become frustrated. They need more patience for slow learners; these people are stopping them from achieving their goals and being able to move on.

Protectors like to be efficient. If a meeting has been scheduled for a specific time, turn up on time. If people are tardy, expect a dressing down or a veiled, sarcastic comment in front of others, regardless of any excuse. They have a point to make.

A Protector provides stability within their family; they desire a secure home and teach their children right from wrong. They are not the most romantic of people; they become comfortable in love and do not 'feel' the need to keep showing it.

'Emotion' is just a word to a transparent-minded Protector; it can get in the way of doing more important stuff. They develop deep relationships with loved ones, but once things are sealed, they do not see the point of constantly exerting effort to remind people of it. They need to be asked to show emotion; their feelings run deep, and they can be hurt, but they will not show it publicly.

A stressed Protector results in a criticising Protector. This usually happens when the rules are not being followed or when they allow people to misinterpret them. Protectors prefer to work in the 'black and white' of guidelines and find operating in the grey areas difficult. The deeper they go into the grey, the less efficient they become and the more adverse they become to decision-making.

Protectors love a good plan and are very quick to pull a lousy situation apart, understanding it and then being able to reevaluate, giving a clear direction. They can constantly develop a plan, and once it has been formulated, they will follow it, regardless of any problems. Being quite stubborn, they will only change their mind when it is proven that another way is more efficient and uses better resources.

If a Protector makes a mistake, you do not need to worry about trying to soften the blow. Take them somewhere private; the most crucial thing is quickly getting to the point! Tell them what the mistake was and prepare to argue the fact. Have some examples and evidence ready, and once they have had a chance to digest the feedback, they will accept it.

They will often thank you and expect to be allowed to correct matters.

Upsetting a Protector is easy; break a promise or an agreement, and watch them hit their button. Not doing something that has been agreed upon is a deal-breaker. They use trust in most negotiations, and if trust has been abused, a Protector has a long memory. They can and will refer to specific incidents, justifying why they do not have faith in someone. It will take months of effort for someone to prove their worth again, so it would be easier not to upset a Protector in the first place.

If a Protector is upset, leave them to their thoughts and get out of their way. They will not explode but become angry and snap if you get too close. Do not think they need their hands held or a shoulder to cry on; this will not help the situation. Only once they have calmed down will they seek someone to talk to, but they will only confide in people they trust. Space and time are the best medicine for dealing with an upset Protector.

Protectors don't always stay focused until a task is complete. They can start to procrastinate if they do not have time to finish a task, and they will delay starting tasks if it means they must stop halfway through one due to things like time or lack of supplies. They would much rather complete it in one go than take a break overnight and finish it later.

Protectors are control freaks. They like to be challenged by being given increasingly more complex tasks. They see these assignments as recognition and acknowledgement of their abilities.

Protectors cannot hide their frustration and can be seen as aggressive and fiery individuals. People who do not know them will stay away because Protectors frighten them. Those who are used to this persona will be able to see through the frustration and manage the situation better, as they know that there is no harm in these outbursts and that the Protector is just trying to get the job done.

Most people will enjoy the protection a Protector offers, whether they want it or not. People who work within the rules can rely on a protector to be in their corner. Protectors are ferocious supporters.

Protectors like to operate in areas that they are familiar with. If asked to decide on an unknown specialism, they will not hazard a guess and will defer to others. They always prefer to be right; they can only defend their actions if they know their subject. When pushed, they will find a way to delay a response and find the correct reply by asking others or suggesting alternative people to talk to. They will not be drawn into making an instant decision, as this might be wrong.

Tips for Protectors when they deal with the other tribal members.

PROTECTOR VS PROTECTOR

Protectors usually are very good together. They have mutual respect for ethics. They will support another Protector unless they believe they are competing with them. Protectors will want to be in charge, even if everyone within a group is of the same grade. Protectors will not openly undermine each other but will rally support, surrounding themselves with people who will champion their cause. They believe that a larger support group will prove their dominance.

Protectors do not show much emotion; a relationship with another can seem cold and business-like. The house will be well-run and organised. There will be a mutual understanding between them, and one does not need to explain why to the other. They would acknowledge the other's achievements, seeing it as a competition, but will work hard to do something just as recognisable to keep things balanced. Protectors would set a task to become friends; they would schedule a meeting for a coffee, as they would for a weekly squash game. They will pencil something into their diary as long as they do not have to discuss emotions.

Protectors will learn a lot from other Protectors, but only when they concede some authority to the other. The only way they will do this is when there is mutual respect and trust in each other. They find tasks in their personal lives hard, being control freaks; they find it difficult to rely on others to do the right thing, especially when at a social gathering someone else has organised, without their input. In a social environment, they'll be happy to give responsibility to another Protector once they have made sure they have similar standards and are following the expected social etiquette rules, but will struggle with anyone else.

PROTECTOR VS GATHERER

Protectors and Gatherers can be a good relationship as neither will want to deal with emotions. Both are happy to deal with any given task and do not need to use idle chit-chat before they get into it. There is mutual respect for following the rules on both sides. The direct approach of the Protector can make a Gatherer feel undervalued, as they cannot communicate in the same way, especially if they need to defend their actions.

Neither Protectors nor Gatherers worry about pleasantries, and the relationship will be very business-like. Protectors will tend to overrule a Gatherer. Being a control freak, the Protector gives out tasks and a specific set of instructions very bullishly. Gatherers play into this as they like information, and the more information a Protector gives, the more eager a Gatherer will become. A list with long instructions and even a PowerPoint presentation is all a Gatherer wants before they get going, and this is what Protectors love to do: create lists and instructions! However, the Protector will grow tired of the constant need for more information, and frustration can happen when there is no visible progress.

The need for a Gatherer to constantly ask questions, with the 'sky thinking' attitude and "What if..." questions, will push a Protector over the edge. Protectors have a short fuse and believe that too much talking and no action deserves a heavy hand to get things back on track. They may blame a Gatherer, calling them a problem maker, rather than having to talk any more. The Protector will never accept that they have not given clear instructions; they do not understand the Gatherer's need for more and more information. Protectors cannot expect a Gatherer to complete a task quickly. If a Protector knows they are meeting with a Gatherer, they need time to prepare lots of information and handouts. A detailed email sent to a Gatherer before and after a meeting will get things moving quicker, and lots of follow-up communication will keep things moving.

PROTECTOR VS HEALER

Protectors and Healers are the complete opposite of each other, but they complement each other's traits, filling in the gaps for the other. The flexible nature of the Healer means they will go along with suggestions from a strong Protector personality. The Protector, an efficient task-orientated machine and a Healer who sees the good in people and does not want to cause upset, means there is little argument. Healers hearing the importance of a task in the stern tones of a Protector will need little convincing to fulfil such a task. A Protector can burn out Healers and must remember not to overwork a Healer, as they will not say no.

Protectors are not emotional; however, Healers will try to get them to open up and soften them, wanting them to show some friendly affection. Healers need to know what is going on under the tough exterior of a Protector so that they will ask lots of personal questions. Protectors can see this as digging rather than helping; it will get annoying when someone constantly asks, "Are you all right?" as they cannot read any emotion from a Protector. A Protector is incredibly neutral and not interested in friendship dynamics whilst at work; they tend to share more personal thoughts with a Healer, but it must be a genuine friendship. When a friendship no longer works, the Protector will cut all ties, go cold, and let the relationship wilt. The Healer might ask what went wrong, but the Protector will not respond, ignoring questions. This will not change unless that Healer becomes useful again.

A Protector needs to be reminded that Healers are kind-natured, gentle souls. If they want to improve their relationship with a Healer, they need to listen more, not be tempted to jump in to fix it, but just be there. A Protector might also want to open up and give a Healer a personal story to show that they trust the Healer.

PROTECTOR VS HUNTER

Protectors see Hunters as 'noise'. They can both get along, but when issues arise, it will be because Hunters have done something. They are seen as jokers. Hunters are not to be trusted with important tasks. Hunters are not serious enough for Protectors, and this will undermine the relationship. Both are high performers, and both get their work done. Hunters do not necessarily stick to the rules, which frustrates the Protectors, especially when they get the same result. Hunters want things to be more fluid, which drives a Protector wild, seeing them as 'flitting' between tasks and not being focused.

Hunters bring Protectors back to humanity, showing there is more to life than work or being task-orientated. They can release a Protector from the daily grind of completing task after task. Protectors

THE CAVEMAN PRINCIPLES

will only stand so much messing around from a Hunter; their short fuse can regularly be lit by all the laughter and fun a Hunter brings to the party. The fallout between them can be pretty short, with a Protector wanting to get back on task, and the Hunter will barely blink, water off a duck's back attitude, as there won't be a prolonged dispute. They can both find common ground quickly, getting on with things.

The Protector will have to engage with the Hunter's emotions, as the Hunter will push them down their throats. The Hunter is the only other tribe member who can and will tell a Protector how it is. This partnership will make a Protector more rounded and less sharp. Feedback between the two can be brutal but necessary. Hunters and Protectors make brilliant companions. Protectors will quickly recognise Hunter's unusual task approach and credit them if they continually get good results. Hunters have skills and abilities that a Protector can use, especially the no-fear aspect and the desire to get on with a task. The biggest reason they fallout is when the Protector does not give enough praise and recognition.

9.
GATHERERS

Tell me more, and don't spare any details.

Gatherers being both Closed and Indirect, are unique characters. The tribe member closest to the Earth element. Our ancestral Cavemen Gatherers were the cautious ones in the group. They would be suspicious of everything and everyone, whether they were friends, foes, or unknowns, no one was ever fully trusted. Gatherers would never have put themselves in harm's way unless they had no other choice, and even then, some risk assessment would have been done. A Gatherer probably thought up the first 'Health and Safety' rules and then went around training people how to handle fire before they had a chance to discover it.

Gatherers were the sensible members of the tribe. They stood back, watched people fail, and took notes on how not to do it, not wanting to end up on 'CaveTube fails'. They planned how to do it properly and relished telling others about their mistakes.

THE CAVEMAN PRINCIPLES

Cavemen Gatherers would have their days planned, including what time to get up, where they were going, and what they would do. They ensured everything on their to-do list was done before they got an early night.

They would have been the first to have worked out the best sleeping position and tried several places to ensure it was. For safety reasons, they probably were not the first ones out of the cave each day but the second or third. They enjoyed the same routines and the same safe, monotonous lifestyle. They did not like change. They were happy that they knew what they were doing and did it repeatedly, day after day.

The Gatherers probably kept the tribe ticking over, getting all the menial, tedious tasks done, such as collecting water, firewood, and berries. They got on with it with little complaint, and their actions went unnoticed. They did not need praise, as completing the task and doing it the right way was all that was required.

Gatherers wanted the tribe to be an efficient and safe place to live. They planned the future, made rules and policies, and ensured everyone knew them. They could have been seen as busybodies; however, people appreciated their input once they realised their purpose.

Gatherers had a trust issue. They trusted only themselves and those who had proved loyalty and worthiness. They were happy to be loners. They would leave the cave, go foraging alone, and not need a team to motivate them. They knew what they were looking for and did not need someone interfering in their work. They would only be looking for their tried-and-tested foods, wanting to avoid trying new berries, plants, or other foreign things that could be eaten.

Gatherers would bring back just enough food for the tribe to eat and be satisfied. They did not waste effort or resources to get as much food as possible, as they understood rationing and shortages. Their careful planning dictated how much they should use and how many berries they needed. They would not want to waste their hard work gathering if it did not benefit them or the tribe.

Gatherers were forward planners, probably collecting sticks and bits of wood, thinking these items might be handy if the tribe invented something like fire. This was the level of eventuality Gatherers would have been planning for. They were the "Yes, but..." tribe members, always trying to cover every angle.

Modern-day Gatherers still have the same traits, but now with less of an overbite and access to an iPad or tablet that displays their 'To Do' list. They check results and record things as they go, which must have a purpose and be worthy of their effort.

Gatherers love a good process. They love Spreadsheets even more. They are the happiest when they follow a pre-planned process that will deliver the same result time after time. Not a fan of change or any new process, Gatherers need so much detail that no one can supply the quantity they need before they deviate. The more information they can gather about a process, the more comfortable they will be with it.

As Gatherers like to keep their feet on the ground, they are the 'Earth' types. They are happy to continue with things because they can access ongoing information. This chapter is purposefully a bit longer for that very reason. If Gatherers learn enough from this book, they will be more comfortable living the Caveman Principles. They need the extra input to have more examples of how it works and even to repeat specific scenarios for them to appreciate the benefits.

Gatherers need to collect as much raw data as possible from various sources. They may have already read loads of books about identifying personality types. They want all routes, avenues, roads, footpaths, bridleways, shortcuts, and tunnels covered. This group is the "What if..." crowd. With enough knowledge, they believe they can cover all eventualities.

With a drive to be so well informed, they can go for years, covering hundreds of sources, books, and web searches before they make an informed choice. They do not understand gut instinct and dislike being forced into making quick decisions. They must be allowed time to make these decisions.

Otherwise, they will push their button and refuse, screaming that they cannot do it. They hate making mistakes and are the deepest of reflectors. Gatherers need thinking stages to digest, assess, and use all the information they have gathered. They are considered ' difficult ' when they delay giving an opinion or a direction. When a quick or straightforward decision is needed, others can get very irate with Gatherers; they can be said to have 'no backbone' and are unwilling to take any form of risk or a gamble. It takes hours or even days to decide the best course of action, but this is how they operate: slow, methodical and entirely rational. They need space to make the right decision; if not given, they get stressed and withdraw.

In the police, there were several 'gatekeepers'; they reviewed the evidence and decided if we should charge people with an offence and send them to court. I quickly realised that out of the four people who did this role, two were Protectors, one was a Healer, and the one with the immense piles of case files around their desk was a Gatherer. I only gave work to the Gatherer when the things I investigated were so severe, or I had something else I could get on with whilst they deliberated over things. Otherwise, my caseload would have been unmanageable.

When Gatherers are allowed the time to make an informed decision, they are steadfast in their final judgment. They will have put much work into the task and would have covered all eventualities, making their case watertight. If their decision is ever challenged, they will have gathered so much data to prove their theory that most people's questions have already been thought of and mitigated. Most of their offence charge decisions made it to court and typically had a positive outcome.

When a Gatherer is ready to give information, they are the ones who state, "Tell them what you are going to tell them, tell them and then tell them what you have told them." This information delivery style is widely accepted as the 'briefing model', but Gatherers love it because they get three chances to give a well-thought-out reason. Gatherers are indirect regarding their need to be forthright unless there is a process they can hide behind. They struggle to get straight to the point and will build up an entire story before they can deliver their message within that telling. Being that they are matter-of-fact, they can seem unemotional, but they also appreciate not wanting to get into an argument, so their feedback can be unique and get lost in translation.

Gatherers will have a wealth of knowledge on a given subject, especially one they enjoy. If they believe that someone is doing something wrong in a work topic they know, they get irate about it. They become difficult and hostile as they do not know how to interject. Instead, they worry about the result and challenge how it is done. Instead of challenging the work, they throw rules, laws and regulations at people, expecting them to know what they have done wrong and that this logical approach will correct the problem.

Gatherers hate change, but as an oddity, they love new technology if it does not change what they already know. If they see learning about a new gadget as worthwhile, they will go beyond the manual, almost infatuated with it. Gatherers learn best through reading and research. They will research to find something that their peers do not know.

Gatherers do not make impulsive purchases. When making purchases, they explore the best option and where to buy it. Price is just one factor for a Gatherer; they will also look at the best guarantee, service cover, and customer feedback.

Once they have chosen where to get their new piece of kit, which will take some time, they will double-check before whipping out the credit card (which they would have also researched for the best rates and rewards).

Unlike the other tribe members, when Gatherers get their newly purchased item home, they cannot wait to read the instructions. They read them cover to cover before taking the gadget out of the box. This will be done for the most complex systems and even for a simple toaster or kettle.

For Gatherers, there is always something to learn. They get comfort from pages and pages of information, even if most will be irrelevant. They can consume data, store it and use it or refer to it in the future.

Gatherers learn best through reading information. They need to gain a firm grasp of the facts, but they will still want to know where to ask questions to confirm their understanding.

Gatherers do not understand why people wouldn't want to sit through five hours of PowerPoint presentations for a simple training session. They love seeing the words on a screen and being told them. They love to ponder instructions slowly and would do anything to slow down a session to prolong any helpful input.

If a person were to ask a question at the end of a training session, you could put money on the questioner being a Gatherer. Their thought process can identify the start of a Gatherer's question, as it always starts with, "What if…." or "Just to clarify…" They cannot remain silent when allowed to ask a question; they see it as a chance to grab more information and clarify any ambiguities. They enjoy staying behind, speaking with the trainer at the end of a session, and trying to glean any extra content or knowledge from them.

Gatherers learn much faster when a process is taught through a structured plan. They also need to manage when much information is just thrown at them. They take loads of notes at meetings and will have pages of references from any training they attend. They take it away to work through it all at their own pace and research areas where they need clarification.

THE CAVEMAN PRINCIPLES

Gatherers are naturally gifted strategists. The 'Games Workshop', where Warhammer and other games are played by Henry Cavill (yes, another DC superhero gets a mention), will be full of Gatherers. These types of strategy-based games allow the player to think five steps ahead. The game allows sufficient time to make reasoned choices and gives the player space to assess each move. Gatherers also enjoy games like chess and Monopoly, dragging games out for hours as they think about their next move.

Gatherers tend to stand out from the bulk of a tribe as they can be seen as slightly different. This is partly because they are closed and choose not to mix with the rest of the tribe. Gatherers prefer their own company or the company of other Gatherers. They do not need social interaction from anyone and prefer being alone rather than putting up with someone who does not think the same way.

Gatherers are, by their nature, knowledge seekers; they trust genuine information, proven facts and trusted sources. They do not understand or can accept the notion of a gut feeling, especially when important decisions must be made. They rely on logical thought processes, following known facts.

Their head leads everything they do, not their heart. If a group votes on a potential outcome that cannot be proven or appears to be the right choice for a group without facts, then Gatherers will not want to be part of it.

When Gatherers learn a new process, they experiment and test elements of it until they fully trust it. They will only use it when they have proven that it all works. They will try to incorporate a new process into other working methods, but only if they think it enhances their status as the knowledge hub. Another sign you are speaking to a Gatherer is their work and personal email signature block; it will be long and full of information no one will read or use. It will give loads of different ways to contact them (rather than people just wanting to push the reply button) that others will never use. Over time, you can compare its growing length and detail, and there will be a marked comparison.

Gatherers enjoy known processes and are resistant to new ideas. They dislike change, which needs to be assessed. They do not use unproven theories. Before they accept a new process, they carefully evaluate and experiment with everything about it.

As Gatherers follow processes, they can be seen as unyielding, refusing to deviate from original plans or rejecting new working methods. They try to make a new scenario fit into a tried and tested process rather than making a new process to accommodate a new scenario. They may get mixed results, but they know where a process needs to be monitored and modified. Others will criticise their efforts because they do not understand that a Gatherer needs to follow a process. Gatherers can change, but it will be a slow progression.

Gatherers are the 'belt and braces' thinkers. They will exceed the requirements when completing any task. Rather than sticking to a ' that will do ' attitude, they would write a page justifying their overly complex process. Simple one-word answers such as "Yes" are not part of a gatherer's thought process, and simple tasks like emptying a bin can take hours.

Going to the cinema is more than turning up at the start of a movie. They will check all timings, such as when it starts and ends. They will check where the best seats are in the theatre, which cinema has the best deal and how they will get there. If they stick to their schedule, they will have a wonderful time.

However, if there are any delays or other people are late, they will be pushing their button, and the experience will be awful. When a Gatherer finds a new process, rather than have it imposed on them, they go through the motions of proving that it works, but they will slot this in between their daily tasks and find it a chore. They will use it whenever they can if they believe it benefits them. Gatherers even bolt on a valid process at the end of another helpful process. They probably invented double bagging for their shopping, even for a single loaf of bread. These double- and even triple-checked processes mean they are incredibly risk-averse, and whatever they do, any potential mistake has been mitigated and minimised.

A bunch of Gatherers probably championed the inception of a Health and Safety set of rules. It makes perfect sense that many risk-averse, process-driven individuals want to prevent all eventualities from ever happening. The details about operating any machine, tool, or environment can and will reduce accidents, which is a Gatherer's dream exercise. The fact that all Gatherers will firmly accept is that due to the efforts of people being able to cover all aspects of dangerous situations, the introduction of health and safety legislation has dramatically reduced the number of deaths and serious injuries. Spelt out, this means someone researched it and put a plan into action, and it has the results to back it up, proof that it works.

Gatherers like writing long, detailed emails with an oversized signature block at the bottom (most of its content being copied and pasted from somewhere), and the message seems over the top. They would read the entire message and expect others to do the same. They would spend a lot of effort preparing the message for the recipient, believing it is all there for a purpose - justification. Gatherers need to get to the point. Instead, they hide information in text, so someone must read the entire message. While reading, the clever Gatherer will have placed reasoned arguments on either side of the information, supporting their decision to reduce people's misunderstanding of what has been written.

Gatherers are meticulous, explaining why they must learn every process before they give it a go. If the process is long, detailed and staged, they excel at getting it right the first time. They might not be the fastest at completing a task, but their understanding of each step before they jump in will mean that they will have consistent results, and due to their knowledge, they become the ideal trainer. With no shortcuts, if a process needs to be taught to someone, a Gatherer is the right person to do it.

Gatherers are determined. They rely on facts, as facts and hard evidence can never be wrong! Once a Gatherer has made their mind up, they become strong-willed, and it becomes very difficult to convince them otherwise. They go through a long mental process, weighing up the odds, foreseeing different outcomes, and settling on the perfect process, so change will not happen instantly.

Gatherers are indirect, and as they always want things to be correct, they need help trusting non-Gatherers to follow the proper process. They don't delegate, often preferring to complete the task themselves. Due to not getting to the point quickly, they can seem a little wishy-washy. They get frustrated at being unable to voice their concerns and can be seen as rude, especially when they want to challenge someone who has not done a 'prescribed' task correctly.

THE CAVEMAN PRINCIPLES

They struggle to turn a blind eye to bad work, and it can push their button. They correct people by shouting policy and 'accepted' standards at them.

When a Gatherer believes that a specific process is not being followed, they can't help but interfere. They don't worry about hurting someone's feelings if a process needs correcting. They have been known to take over the task to ensure it gets done right, ignoring the other person's frustrations—task over feeling—even when they cannot find time to manage the task.

Gatherers can get so focused on a process that they can forget they are dealing with humans who have emotions and feelings. They do not mean to be rude as they concentrate on a task instead of being people-focused. Gatherers apply themselves to learning and then enjoy teaching those skills. Even if the person with whom they want to teach does not want their input, they will still preach the right way to do things. This is a strong moral obligation to a Gatherer, as they want to ensure it is done right.

Gatherers believe that being an 'area' specialist will give them more authority and a chance for promotion, and they expect it to be based on their key performance indicators. This is why they become obsessed with one area of work, record their achievements, and push others to make them look good.

Gatherers enjoy having complete control of a task, especially when they get to be the only ones involved. They are more relaxed on their own than part of a team. They have trust issues in other people's abilities, finding it hard to believe that other people's work is up to their standard. They feel uncomfortable when they cannot check if a process has been followed properly. For this reason, a Gatherer will micromanage any task. They constantly need feedback and reassurance to ensure a process is followed correctly; updates and progress reports are daily requirements. They offer 'helpful' advice as they want the job completed correctly.

Gatherers need thinking time to complete any task; otherwise, they do not function properly, pushing their buttons when asked to do a 'rush' job. They need exact figures and do not like it when people use the best guesstimates. If they are handed a completed portfolio and cannot check where the details were obtained, they will need to double-check the figures and check all the facts—needing to be fully satisfied that the entire job was done correctly.

Gatherers are great process managers. They do not get emotional; they are perfect for managing a production line. They expect everyone to conform to the same 'acceptable standard', and these standards are rigorously checked. They get annoyed when people bring personal issues into the workplace. They find it hard to understand why people's problems can't just stay at home.

Gatherers struggle to understand what they cannot control. Emotions cannot be quantified, so they shy away from anything related to a sensitive matter unless it is gossip, which they can fact-check and store for later use.

Gatherers tend to avoid going to social gatherings. They need to see the benefit of going out in their time to mix with people with whom they could chat in the office.

Unless there is a personal benefit to attending a social meeting, such as speaking to a manager at a barbecue or having a free lunch, they would prefer to stay away.

Gatherers are good at weighing up probabilities and looking for logical outcomes. They enjoy finding mistakes or errors and feel their role is highlighting them to others. To try and understand how a Gatherer thinks, imagine seeing 'time' as a sequence of many events, all colour-coded and categorised, then filed away in a logical order rather than a smooth-flowing timeline full of experiences. Hopefully, you can start to understand how they operate.

Gatherers believe they will always be right because they follow a tested and trusted system. They appear amazingly calm when others are in stressful situations, even when they seem unable to grasp the full extent of the circumstances. This non-show of emotion gives the Gatherer a bad reputation for not understanding the seriousness of an event, but what they are doing is putting effort into concentrating and finding a resolution, one problem at a time.

The only time a Gatherer loses their cool in a stressful situation is when they are lost, with no information, no process to follow, and no idea where to go for help. They show no emotion; they appear to tread water, getting anxious and fiery while they plan their next move.

If a Gatherer is pushed for an immediate decision, they will panic, and stress buttons will be pressed. They will try to delay an answer, find time to think, make excuses, and ask for answers to pointless questions, as these are all good gatherer distractions. They need to get somewhere away from it all; for some thinking time, they must ponder all the possible outcomes. I have found a Gatherer hiding under their desk with their fingers in their ears, trying to get some alone time.

Gatherers do get angry, but they rarely show it. If they lose their cool and start to shout, they show their frustration at the situation and not normally at the person. To find a Gatherer shouting is rare; they prefer to talk at people instead. They bombard them with logical facts, weaving in a point they are trying to make but not making it too obvious.

A Gatherer does not settle old scores; instead, they make mental records of the wrongs carried out against them, only to be used later when they deem appropriate. They would rather stop interactions with someone and ignore them than carry on with any mistrust they might have. They feel they are proving a point by withdrawing from a task and refusing to cooperate with people who have upset them. They want people to see that their withdrawal from a task is important and that it will prove that, without their help, it will fail. They may even attempt to sabotage the task, throwing in a few spanners and a little discord amongst the remaining team.

Gatherers respond well when asked for advice, especially if they are referred to as specialists or because they have been recognised as having experience in a specific area.

A report written by a Gatherer will be long, containing lots of big, important 'buzz' words. Gatherers think, "Why restrict yourself to five words when fifty conveys the same point?" The bigger, longer and more complex a word is, the Gatherer feels it worthy and should be used. They can write complex reports and fill them with facts, explaining why they are making them so complex and why they need to be fully understood.

Gatherers are incredible parents who look out for their family. They push people to become self-reliant and provide the tools and experience. They teach fact and reason, making their parenting skills a process rather than an emotional and confusing time for themselves and their children.

When they start conversations, they expect them to be about a process rather than a thought. They will bring up obscure facts, justifying their reason. They hope to be allowed to go on about it, getting excited about the details. They expect their audience to appreciate their knowledge.

Gatherers cannot say no to extra work. They take on more tasks than they can handle, believing they are asked because they are the only ones who can do it. Giving a Gatherer a task must have a specific outcome; otherwise, work will start once they clarify what is needed. They do not like things that can change. They want an agreed-upon outcome and prefer avoiding it when people try to change the scope or desired result. A Gatherer will be prepared to scrap an entire project, preferring to restart from scratch rather than modify any part of ongoing work. Gatherers are good at repressing their emotions, and stressed Gatherers can continue to work on a given task, but they become more demanding of others. More questions or micro-managing processes that others are doing. They are unaware of their impact and annoyance of others; even when pointed out, they will believe they are just doing their job. When a Gatherer is stressed, they are intolerant of other people's 'stupidity'.

If a Gatherer needs to be challenged for underperforming or doing something wrong, be prepared for a real fight. Information, facts, evidence, and figures will be required before they accept it. It will need to be spelt out in a logical and chronological order. If they take the findings, they must be shown where they went wrong and want help amending a broken process. They will quickly adapt and move on.

Criticising a Gatherer in an open environment where others will hear is not a good plan; they need a confidential space. Shouting at a Gatherer is pointless; forcing too many changes on them will push their button. Patience and understanding are the keys to getting a Gatherer to change.

Tips for Gatherers, when they deal with the other tribal members.

GATHERER VS GATHERER

Gatherers have a healthy respect for each other. They both understand the importance of discussing a process before starting a task. A pair of Gatherers will not be the fastest, but they will be the most thorough. They make plans and discuss many ways to approach a task before they start. Once they agree on the correct process, they will be happy to get on with things. This type of planning takes time and documentation, and along with their meticulous eye for detail, their scheduling will take longer than most. However, they are almost guaranteed to deliver on their time scale and budget, and the result will be to everyone's satisfaction. There will be plenty of progress reports and documentation of the outcome.

Gatherers are entirely status-orientated. If they both believe they are more experienced, it will cause problems. Being closed, they will not be able to discuss this with each other, and neither will be forthright enough to broach the subject. They will nitpick and expect the other to fall into place, acknowledging this status without the need to challenge the other. Problems can happen when one has already secured a plan, and if a latecomer wants to change part of it, then expect tantrums. There is no fighting; they will talk 'at' each other, trying to convince the other to change because they are superior.

If two Gatherers go for the same promotion, they will become dirty, recording each other's failures with evidence of poor decision-making. This is to put the other down rather than lift themselves up. There is no subtlety in using this tactic, and when one starts, the other will follow, and things will get out of hand.

If Gatherers fall out with each other, it will be their change in status, with the other not accepting it. They will ignore or make snide remarks at each other until they regain an equal standing. The quickest way to get Gatherers over an upset is to mediate between them, and even though they may accept it, they will always hold a grudge.

GATHERER VS HEALER

Gatherers and Healers are both Indirect. Neither will push the other around, and both will be pretty respectful of each other. A Gatherer will see a Healer as someone who is 'away with the fairies', flitty and unfocused. Healers trust their emotions and gut feelings too much rather than a carefully thought-out plan. Healers tend to support Gatherers as they do not like upsetting people, and they would rather give in than fight with someone who appears to have a factual and well-structured plan.

Gatherers who are not open will be uncomfortable sharing personal thoughts and feelings with a Healer. If asked about how they feel, even just once, their perception will be that they are being constantly asked. Gatherers will get tetchy, and a Healer will feel compelled to keep asking, as there is no resolve. A loop can occur, with the Gatherer trying anything to avoid answering, calling the question a distraction and a waste of time, rather than opening up and being honest about things. A Healer will see a Gatherer as needing help and will keep trying. However, a Gatherer will win as they are more headstrong, and the Healer will eventually give up. Gatherers have been known to ignore Healers and even avoid them to avoid these questions. The Healer's feelings will get hurt, but they should get over it, yet a Gatherer will feel uncomfortable for quite some time afterwards.

If a Gatherer needs to improve the relationship with a Healer, they must open up, become more of a friend, and show that they trust them. A Healer finds it hard to ignore someone who is so insular, so sharing some personal thoughts with them will make a big difference. Healers do not like lots of information, but they do listen, so information delivery needs to be spoken; throw in some emotion, and a Healer will get on board very quickly. Gatherers need to learn to say thank you and "I feel..." for a Healer to be happy, stopping Healers feeling they are being taken for granted.

GATHERER VS HUNTER

Gatherers are so focused on a process that having a lively Hunter around will get them to press their buttons quickly. These two personalities will likely clash and even fight over something others think is just a storm in a teacup. Hunters can get under the skin of a Gatherer, and when a Gatherer gets upset, they will shout and start to fill with frustration very quickly. On the other hand, Hunters will treat this as a game, enjoying winding up the Gatherer even further, not knowing the volcano they keep poking. After a while, the Gatherer tries to ignore them; this should be a warning, the calm before the storm, but as the fun has stopped, the Hunter will start to get frustrated and push harder. When the Hunter loses their temper, they will want an open and frank discussion with the Gatherer about what happened; this is when the Gatherer explodes.

If a Gatherer can use and hone a Hunter's productive attitude, they will get excellent results. Providing that both are willing to give a little, the coupling of these two can be a fantastic mix; with the pace at which the Hunter works and the Gatherer's skill in reporting, this can impress many people. To achieve this, they must be kept separated, with little contact. If the Gatherer has no idea of what the Hunter is doing, this will cause problems, so having short, regular catch-up meetings will be of benefit. If a Gatherer can separate a task into the thinking and the doing side, not straying into the Hunter's territory, they can work peacefully together. The real issue is that Hunters despise being micromanaged, whereas Gatherers find comfort in knowing every step is followed correctly. A Gatherer should not inspect a Hunter's work whilst in front of them; there will be criticism, and the Hunter will not tolerate it. The Hunter would not be interested in inspecting the Gatherer's work, as it is not their style, so there will be no exchange.

When a Gatherer needs to improve a relationship with a Hunter, take them out for a beer. Getting them to meet socially will get them to let their guard down, and they might realise they like each other. Hunters need to feel connected to people, so they communicate with them, probably far too much for a Gatherer's liking. When things get too much for a Gatherer, they need to explain this. Telling a Hunter they must prepare a PowerPoint presentation will do the trick. The Hunter will not ask questions, go quiet, and the Gatherer will be free to leave.

GATHERER VS PROTECTOR

Interactions between Gatherers and Protectors are usually quite good. They both like quantifiable results and focus on getting things right the first time. A Gatherer would instead take their time at the beginning, getting things in place, whereas a Protector does not like to waste time discussing the best option. They want to make a quick decision and will want to get on with things, assessing the progress as they go. Gatherers are like Protectors as they do not allow emotions to get in the way of a task. The pair can become task-orientated and complete their tasks to a high standard, but this attitude can alienate others.

Gatherers need to get on with pushy Protectors; these are the ones who put short deadlines on tasks, not giving room to think about things, and this can push buttons. Any Gatherer that needs to confront a Protector will not be able to do so, as most Protectors are far too stern for their liking. They prefer to avoid confrontational conversations, as Protectors can be short and not allow them to explain themselves fully. Gatherers could be more adept at handling strong-willed Protectors as they can easily be beaten into submission. The Protector's more dominant, direct nature can win every conversation, so instead, a Gatherer will start to withdraw and try to pass the task on to someone else.

If a Gatherer needs to improve a relationship with a Protector, they must stand up for themselves. Becoming a more forthright individual will catch the

Protector's attention, showing the Protector that the Gatherer can make quick decisions and, therefore, is a worthy adversary. Gatherers being more direct about what they want will be uncomfortable, but this is the only way to gain recognition and grow a better relationship. Gatherers must show the Protector they have some 'Grrrrrr' in them. Earning the respect of a Protector takes time, consistency and perseverance, but as soon as change starts to happen, it will take hold quite quickly.

THE CAVEMAN PRINCIPLES

10.
HEALERS

How are you feeling?

Healers are both Open and Indirect. They have the closest traits associated with the Water element. Our ancestral Caveman Healers would have been the first aiders in the tribe. Their caring nature meant they were perfect for getting the sick and wounded back on their feet. They would have liked to be around people, especially those who needed them. The tribe would have accepted the role of a Healer as the go-to person. When someone needed to talk or just a little TLC, the Healer would be singled out. The Healer just wanted everyone to be healthy and happy. Healers were the 'people pleasers' of the tribe. Healers were the ones that the tribe turned to when they wanted someone to understand them.

They were the ones who knew everyone's worries. Healers were the gentle, kind and approachable individuals within the tribe. Undoubtedly, their caring attitude would have been taken advantage of by a few of the other tribe members, but they would not have taken it personally. They would have been easy targets for practical jokes and would have been easily swindled.

Healers generally have the 'nice guy' outlook on life. This comes from their openness towards others, combined with their indirect communication style, which means they do not want to upset anyone. They would have made brilliant tribal teachers and wonderful mentors. Their willingness to help others would be used to teach children how to hunt, protect, gather, and heal.

Healers would be the most knowledgeable, as they would have made the effort to understand the principles of the other trades of the tribe. They may have lacked the desire to do many tasks the others performed, but they could have taught and passed this basic understanding on to those who wished to learn to use them. They would have been trusted to bless the luck of a hunt or ceremonies that the clergy would perform today. Their unbiased outlook, not wanting to take sides, would have been widely used as a mediator or negotiator between members and other tribes.

Even though most modern-day Healers no longer have grazed knuckles and might be able to operate a Breville sandwich toaster (but not bright enough to prevent burning their tongue on the hot cheese), they have managed to keep the same qualities as their much older cousins. Healers look for friendship and are often found sitting on the fence when taking sides in an argument, wanting to try to appease both sides.

They are open and will be pretty sociable to maximise their chances of making new friends. They are the ones who usually organise the work's Christmas meals and then look after the group, especially the stragglers or the quiet ones, trying to get them involved. It is always an excellent plan to take a Healer or two on a pub crawl, as it guarantees people will get home in one piece. Healers love to be part of a group and can chat about anything. They enjoy listening to others and being part of 'something' bigger.

Healers like to look for problems that they think they can fix. They try to read situations to ensure people are happy and having a good time. They are the ones constantly asking, "Are you OK?" They have a deep personal drive to ensure people are well looked after and cared for.

THE CAVEMAN PRINCIPLES

Healers are wonderful friends to many people. They are great counsellors who love hearing about other people's troubles. They are always willing to give helpful, kind support to anyone who needs it. They are like the Water element, washing away troubles and always being calm in their appearance when they help. A Healer will always be available to go for a pint; they will drop whatever they are doing to meet up, especially if someone says they need their help. They are the person that people call when they are feeling down or when things are not going as planned. Healers are trustworthy and are not interested in spreading gossip; they are excellent secret keepers.

Healers are invested in personal growth and often reinvent themselves, sporting new hairstyles and clothing or finding new places to visit. They enjoy social occasions and will be the first to respond to any invitation.

Healers test themselves, driving themselves to be better friends. They are the most sensitive tribe member in the group, picking up signals from those being slightly hostile toward them or others. They can be hard to spot as they will change their behaviour to become more likeable, even if it goes against their beliefs. They prefer to fit in rather than stand out. They strive to make other people's lives better, as everyone deserves to be happy, and they are prepared to do this even if they are put out or it causes them some upset. They are out there, imaginative thinkers and can be found daydreaming with all sorts of wonderful, lovely thoughts going through their minds. This is how they release their tension; meditation is their medicine.

Healers are interested in health and psychology, learning new ways to help others. Their desire to be seen as kind and helpful pushes them onto a more 'spiritual' path. This boosts their caring image, but others in the tribe can see them as being a bit too 'hippy'. Healers do not like bad news; they will be the first to reply to a negative social media status with "What's up mate?" They genuinely want to know if they can help rather than dig for gossip.

Healers have big hearts and see the world as a good place to live. Some may think this is a liberal attitude, but they see bad people as having good souls who made a few bad choices. When Healers see suffering in the world, they feel pain. They like to do things that can help, such as volunteering for a cause. They may support several charities, happy to collect money by singing in a bath full of beans or joining in foolhardy adventures, all because they believe in the cause. Healers can be found standing in public places, outside supermarkets, holding charity boxes, or chasing people around an office to sign their latest sponsorship form.

Healers take a holistic view of negative events; they believe in 'cause and effect'. They want to solve the world's hunger problems, give water to Africa, and treat every disease by raising money for them. They will plant rhubarb in their garden, giving it to friends and neighbours. They will go over the top regarding recycling, and their attempt to show they are saving the planet can be annoying.

Healers do not like to take sides as they want to be everyone's friend. This can upset some friends, who believe that a Healer should only be loyal to them.

Healers want recognition for being unbiased, so they will not be asked to take a side. They want to be seen as the only person who can speak to both parties, enjoying being the mediator.

When a Healer has been wronged, they see it as a breach of trust and expect others to take their side, as they are the lovely party. Those who choose the other side are also cut off.

Healers have deep emotions and are very fragile. Healers can easily be hurt if accused of being nasty or uncaring. Healers view emotions like riding a roller coaster; they always go up and down, but this is where they find true friendships. They are swift to pick up on other people's emotions and match them to their feelings, creating bonds with people much quicker than others. They trust intuition and their gut instinct more than most, often being 'bang on the money' in getting things right. They like being right; it saves upsetting people when they have to apologise. They will not offer an opinion if they are unsure about a subject. A Healer's apology is always lengthy, heartfelt and genuine if it needs to be.

Healers look for deep, meaningful relationships, and when they look for a partner or even a true friend, they want someone with whom they can connect for many years. When they find their soulmate, they lavish attention and love on them like no other tribe member can. This can seem stifling at times, but it means they have found someone they are prepared to spend a lot of time and effort on; going overboard with all the fuss and attention is part of how they show affection and devotion.

Healers see everyone as equals and have no problem with those in authority. They are so involved with emotions that they can come across as impulsive, yet their hearts will always be in the right place.

Parent Healers are the most caring and loving tribal members; they only want what is best for their offspring. They believe that being nice teaches their children ethics and manners, which will, in turn, make them more caring. A Healer does not want to chastise a child. Instead, they will encourage them to work it out for themselves, helping them find their personality by trial and error. When their child has done something wrong, they would rather talk about the hurt it has caused and how it affects their trust rather than shout and scream. They can play for hours with their children, never getting bored. They become engrossed in imaginative play, building a blanket den or a tree house or fighting dragons to get out of a castle; they are just a big kid deep within their core.

Healers need a positive work environment. They can be a source of positive energy, always looking to cheer people up and help explain that things are not as bad as they seem. They act as counsellors within a team, a source of human understanding. They are the ones who others will go to when they feel bad about something; they are the trouble-soothers.

These people-pleasers take on the responsibility of bringing joy to others, volunteering to be the office social organiser, inviting people for end-of-week drinks, putting on a summer barbecue, and ensuring everyone is invited.

The clue is in the term Healers, which can be abundant within the caring profession. Hospitals are full of them, not filling beds but running around looking after the sick and unwell.

They thrive on helping people, so where some humanity is required, a Healer will be close by.

Healers love to learn. Open to trying new things and learning new methods for completing old processes. They become excited while on a training course, knowing they will be better at their job. Healers are auditory learners; they like to discuss new processes and potential ways of working. They learn through communication with open dialogue and discussion, and getting involved in any training aspect is a bonus to them, offering to help others who are struggling. Healers love to hear examples of people's experiences with new ways of working, using them to bolster their enthusiasm for change. They are fascinated by finding out if it works personally and want to discuss how they can include it.

Healers are kind souls who can be taken advantage of and railroaded by stronger tribal characters. It will take a while, but when they realise that they are being used in these circumstances, they feel abused; their pain is real. They will push their button, getting so wound up that they cannot communicate. They dislike people who do not care about them as individuals. They will not shout; instead, they will withdraw, becoming a hermit while they sort out how they feel about things.

Healers put so much effort into helping others that they believe others should do the same in return. They like to play out 'dramas' as a test on their friends. When people ignore their 'life-ending tragedy,' Healers can get incredibly irate. They only want attention and affection from the people they believe are friends. These can be short-lived experiments by them, testing friendships and ensuring their efforts are worthwhile.

If you want to find the Healer of a group, throw an emotional hand grenade into any gathering, declare that you dislike someone who is not there, and then stand back and watch. The one calming everyone down and defending the vulnerable person is your Healer. Asking a Healer to take a side in an argument will also trigger a similar response as they ensure everyone is all right with their choice; they will not want to stand alone or upset anyone. Often, they will wriggle out of making a firm decision, changing the conversation or deliberately being vague to seem unbiased or uncommitted.

Healers do not like people shouting. If a Healer needs to be challenged about their performance, it should not be done publicly; this approach closes them down. They cannot respond when people shout, as they look at the emotion rather than the problem. Speaking to them privately and giving constructive feedback while adding lots of "we" into the conversation, such as "We feel that..." will work much better.

If a Healer becomes upset with someone, they will apologise a lot. Telling others they are sorry for all sorts of things while attempting to quell the anger and not lose their patience. They do not show anger or retaliate like others within the tribe. They bottle up their stress, disappear and cut contact with everyone for a while. Once they calm down, they will reinitiate the relationship but will take things slowly. Even though they are vacant, they will watch from a distance in case they are suddenly needed, and they will appear like a white knight.

Healers do their best when combining imagination, feelings, and intuition. They produce excellent results, but as they go with the flow, they may need help explaining how they achieved an outcome, as they will need help quantifying their actions, other than being able to give the result.

Healers are proud individuals who get insulted when someone does not show respect for their work or asks too many questions, as if someone is picking on their decision, and they feel undermined. They cannot explain their intuition or gut feelings before, during, or after the task, and they expect others to respect the outcome and not dig. If praise is not given or someone attempts to steal the limelight, the Healer will feel undervalued and demotivated, resulting in them not giving their total effort on the next task.

Healers work best when asked to use their recognised skills, especially when they see an opportunity to boost morale. They see themselves as problem removers, resolving emotional issues that allow others to get on with their work. They ask people for opinions and listen to their replies, taking notes and making people feel valued as part of their team. When a Healer feels 'comfortable', they put their entire soul into their work, giving up their time to ensure success. They want to think that something is worth their effort, and they would like acknowledgement from others that they also enjoy the task.

Connecting with a Healer is easy. A handshake is good as they enjoy human contact, but hugging them immediately gets them on board. When they talk directly to people, they want to reach out to touch them, either holding their shoulder or arm, connecting with them as they share an idea. Touching is the quickest way Healers link with others, but they should know when to stop before it goes too far.
Healers keep eye contact with the person they are engaging with. They watch to see if the other person is focused on what is being said, giving extra credit to those who watch their mouth and pick up on body language.

If you need a Healer to pay attention to any specific comment, tell them how positive you feel about the task.

Tips for Healers when they deal with the other tribal members.

HEALER VS HEALER

Healers love to be around their kind. They understand that the world can be lovely and take peace in a caring environment. Through a joint effort, they can make things better; being open and giving emotion encourages them to try harder. Healers attract like-minded souls, sensing each other's openness, they drift in the same direction, meeting at chance opportunities. Quickly recognising these qualities, they easily gain friendship. Healers get on well with one another, yet they tend to separate off, joining groups of other tribal members, probably so they can use their skills on others. When Healers come together, it feels like a supportive and safe environment. They will chat about how they helped others; some may call it gossip, but to them, it is more of a support system, each Healer needing to offload their concerns only to another. They are comfortable knowing that another caring, responsible person will understand the situation, feeling secure in telling others their more intimate secrets.

When a Healer competes with another Healer, they tend to support each other, even holding hands as they cross the finish line. Neither Healer will show a desire to win. Instead, they are supportive of the situation. If they win, they will comfort those behind them instead of celebrating. When Healers get together, they can find something to chat about for hours. They continue until they are completely exhausted or run out of time.

Healers will always support each other and want the best for their friends, even when they do not have the same interests, as it is the emotions they understand rather than the subject. They do not push their agenda. Instead, they ask others for more details, interjecting their thoughts. If a Healer falls out with another Healer, they will not be apart for long unless it is a massive emotional upset. Then the trust has gone, and things are over forever. For minor upsets, they quickly forgive and forget.

HEALER VS HUNTER

Healers and Hunters are very open and enjoy the freedom to use their feelings and emotions in conversations. They can be good friends and work well together. Both are inclined to use gut instincts; they usually get good results, especially when they value the task as worthwhile.

The Hunter will be the more dominant person, applying pressure on the Healer to do it their way. This tends to happen when most of the work has been done, and the Hunter loses interest, needing to finish things, the small details are passed on to the Healer. Healers are happy to finish the task, providing the Hunter will give them credit. A Hunter recognises the Healer's skills, even when there is glory to be received, and the emotional bond is strong enough to ensure this recognition is shared. However, this will only happen if they work together and connect during the task.

Hunters can be dismissive of a Healer, telling them not to bother with the small details, but those last few finishing touches are where a Healer likes to work. When Hunters get bored, they can change the dynamics of a team, burdening the Healer with tedious work, freeing themselves to call the following shots, and moving things along at pace until it gets exciting again. Healers want Hunters to make the same level of commitment in any task, but their intuition allows them to recognise that a Hunter's eye for detail is lacking, and they will happily step up to sort things out.

Suppose a Healer wants to improve a relationship and communication with a Hunter, setting clear boundaries and continually reminding the Hunter when they attempt to change things unnecessarily. Hunters are loyal, but being from the Air element, it is difficult to pin them down; a Healer can run out of patience and give up, so explaining the situation with a Hunter, using emotion, will get things back on track. A Hunter does not do 'subtle', and dropping hints, no matter how big they are, will not be picked up, so tell them exactly how it is. This is outside a Healer's comfort zone, setting boundaries, but the relationship will suffer without them.

Hunters appreciate Healers who can stand up for themselves, do what they are told, and ensure boundaries are not moved.

HEALER VS PROTECTOR

Healers and Protectors are the complete opposite of each other. Yet the dominant Protector against the caring Healer brings a beautiful blend of friendship. If a Healer is being taken advantage of, a Protector has no problem looking after them. A Healer can give emotional guidance to a Protector on subtle matters, softening the Protector's sharp edges; being with them, the Healer makes the Protector more approachable and appear friendly. If they are friends, a Healer can ignore a Protector's blunt questioning and responses, knowing it is not the Protector's intention to be like that. A Healer manages the Protector's stubbornness, as they can make a Protector see reason through sharing emotions. Healers see Protectors as efficient, no-messing individuals, but sometimes they can push the situation when they constantly try to get a Protector to open up.

A Healer and a Protector can have different opinions, which will not affect the dynamics. The Protector will dismiss the Healer's need to feel these things, not being interested in emotion and gut feeling, especially when they make plans. When a Healer thinks a relationship is all 'one-way', they will push their button, wanting to know what the Protector feels about them.

For a Healer to improve a relationship with a Protector, they need to stop worrying about emotions. A Protector only accepts facts, so when they show how unemotional they are, this is a fact and deserves to be retold.

Telling them how their impact affects others will make the point.

Healers who spend time with a Protector will recognise subtle differences in how the Protector deals with others. Everything is black and white, with no grey areas. Although a Protector never seems concerned about how a Healer feels, they need to know that a Healer is part of the team.

If a Healer wants more input from a Protector, they need to ask for it, but get to the point fast and ask a direct question.

HEALER VS GATHERER

Healers and Gatherers are both indirect tribe members.

They both like detail and focus on the small stuff, which others will think is unimportant. The relationship between Healer and Gatherer can be pretty good, providing that the Gatherer does not ask too many "How..." or "What if..." questions. Friction can happen when the openness of a Healer interferes with the closed nature of the Gatherer.

Healers use their emotions and gut instincts far too much for a Gatherer's liking; they want facts. The Gatherer wants a carefully thought-out plan detailing how the Healer will get that result, not the "let's just try" approach that a Healer adapts to. A Healer will not be able to provide the detail a Gatherer wants. Instead, they will be considered as "away with the fairies". If a Healer needs to get on the good side of a Gatherer, they must write stuff down and show a process. A Gatherer needs to pull the result apart, understand it and wants to see the individual functions of each step. This will not be out of spite, but a deep dive into understanding how it was done. Doing this will upset a Healer; they will need to bite their tongue and let it go. These minor misunderstandings can cause genuine upset; the Healer will feel unappreciated, and the Gatherer will not understand how they caused the upset.

If a Healer wants to improve their relationship with a Gatherer, they must develop a logical mindset. If they give running progress updates to a Gatherer, it will stop the Gatherer from being a micro-manager. They will stop interfering and wanting to pull things apart; instead, they will go on the journey and understand the result.

When a Healer needs to write a report or attend meetings run by a Gatherer, they must leave all emotion out of it. Sticking to the facts and projected results, showing processes and how they were obtained, will please a Gatherer. Graphs and references will score points. The Gatherer will see that the Healer is thorough and process-driven, providing the extra leeway they need to manage their work.

11.
GET A TRIBE THAT WORKS

Get the most from your tribe.

People want to feel appreciated, heard and accepted. They thrive in being part of a hard-working, fun and successful tribe. Tribes are full of different types of people. Most of us know that some tribes work better than others, and some don't. There have been occasions when tribes have had such destructive infighting that they get a bad reputation. These bad tribes, if left unchecked, grow and will infect other tribes, and eventually, they will affect an entire organisation, family or social group. Recognition and Action are essential.

Using the Caveman Tribal Sorter, people can recognise character traits within a tribe: the Hunters, Protectors, Gatherers and Healers. Knowing their triggers and exploiting their desires will help improve interactions, grow healthy communication skills, and divert potential problems. Sharing the information in this book will help others understand issues around their personality clashes and help them become more understanding and better tribe members. Personality profiling gets easier with practice, and if people are willing to give it a go, we can all get instant results. Before we dive into team-building exercises, strapping oil drums together and trying to cross a muddy lake, I want to make an essential point about dealing with individuals within a tribe. We use our emotions all the time, and when we want to change something, it is these that we must overcome. The person listening will pick up the undertone rather than the message we want them to think about.

Getting the best out of others is all about communication; when we engage our emotions, we must consider how we come across. Professor Mehrabian has already made this point. He combined two studies and devised a rule about emotions in communication. It is about more than just the spoken or written word; this is only 7% of the interaction. The tone of voice conveys the underlying emotion; its pitch, too loud, soft, too high or too low, accounts for 38%. Then you have the body language, which he stated accounted for the last 55%.

My point is simple. When sending an email to someone, your tone may not be what you think it is. Using 7% of the available communication can lead to disaster, as the other 93% can be 'read between the lines,' and people can get upset over what is not being said. If impact is required when making a statement, human interaction is crucial as it provides the full complement of communication skills; for maximum effect, face-to-face communication is a must, especially for an important matter.

Enough about numbers; we can put our calculators away again. Before we build the perfect tribe, I already know what you are thinking. Filling your tribe with the same character traits as yourself is the easiest thing, as you know what they are like.

I have experience with why we should refrain from using this theory. Years ago, I was part of a police team sent to conduct a last-minute, high-level counterterrorism search operation using some of my specialist training. It was a few days from home, and the work promised to be exciting. With my overnight bags packed, I went to the police yard to find the rest of the team.

At the time, although I knew everyone coming away with me, I had no idea what made them tick.

There was a three-hour drive to our destination, with laughter and high-energy shouting in the back of the van. With hindsight, it was a bunch of Hunters going away. We immediately went to work when we arrived at the 'job'.

Things were great until after the first shift. After completing all the tasks, we cleaned and sealed things up, apart from the paperwork; no one wanted to do it. What we did want to do was tell our 'victory' stories of what we had found. There was some embellishment about how much effort was used, but it made a better story. Things got loud, with people trying to get some praise. It became annoying; people started to get angry, and the paperwork was still unfinished.

After three days, none of us enjoyed each other's company anymore; things had worsened. After finishing the work, there was a silent three-hour journey back to our station. The team could barely say goodbye to each other.

Feelings of resentment were obvious. Three days of just Hunter's interaction had changed everyone's opinions of each other.

Going away with like-minded, similar thought-processing individuals sounded like fun. It should have meant throwing caution to the wind and getting on with the task with little instruction and maximum fun. However, once the glory of the task had been completed, there was no one to clear up after us, and none of us wanted to listen to the exciting stuff anyone else had done.

No one wanted to write the team reports; no one wanted to plan any actions for the next day, what time to meet for breakfast and what time to leave. Although we were always on time and accomplished what we had been asked to do, it was all last-minute stress. It also got repetitive hearing a different version of why "I'm the best" all the time, even when discussing how many sausages someone crammed into their breakfast sandwich. Back in the caveman days, this would have been acceptable, but with rules, regulations and job expectations, things were out of hand.

The same applies to a tribe of Protectors. Even as a team, the individuals take on as many tasks as possible, believing they are the only ones who can do it properly. Without someone with a different outlook focusing on other work areas, these protectors will get 'burnout'. They will snipe at each other for not doing as much as the other, and they will all push buttons. Protectors need to be able to focus on a task to see the result; they need to organise people, not each other. Their achievements need to be acknowledged when it comes to recognition; otherwise, they will lose interest and go elsewhere. A group of Gatherers need too much detail, as much as possible, before they start anything. They become a bunch of procrastinators, meaning vast delays. If you want them to do anything fast, forget it. They will bicker and fight, wanting to get the top spot. It can turn nasty and bitchy, with individual Gatherers going off to do 'their' idea, whether it is part of the plan or not.

Gatherers know their work will be checked. Other Gatherers will inspect the work and find fault, whether they are asked to do so or not. Heavy judgment with a statement to explain will make others very defensive. Overreporting and expecting the worst takes time and has the potential to explode.

Finally, a group of Healers will want to feel part of a team. They will make sure that the others are looked after. None of them will be particularly interested in taking charge, and a certain amount of guesswork and 'gut feelings' will happen. They will be the happiest team, but whatever the amount of work that will be achieved, it will just about be enough.

Modern-day Cavemen can no longer stay within their group, as the world expects more of them. Work has changed; the expectations and demands are more complicated than ever. There is more reporting, more responsibility and more scrutiny than there ever used to be. There is no longer a principal task in any job; employers expect people to fulfil various tasks, needing multi-skilled people with diverse abilities. The jobs of yesteryear are no longer. Instead, organisations have shaved individual roles away from the core of a business, dividing those responsibilities with those who remain, losing the core skill set of the individual role.

People no longer have one responsibility: to go hunting, to watch the tribe, to gather plenty of stocks and supplies and to heal the sick. Today's workers need to be business-focused. In the Police, cops are no longer 'criminal catchers'; they are expected to do the work of social workers, doctors and teachers. They deal with societal issues outside of criminal activity. You need a cop who can fight off 4 attackers (Protectors) and still arrest a violent suspect (Hunter), be able to hold the hand of a domestic violence victim through a complex and unemotional criminal system (Healer) and then be able to be cool, calm and focused to investigate the most difficult of crimes (Gatherer), all these tasks are expected to be completed in just one day.

These professionals need to be lawyers, looking at their reports from every angle in case they get sued (Protectors). Long, unnecessary reports to show they have done their job take time and much deliberation (Gatherers). They have to be ready for the next call (Hunters) and then go home to a loving family that cannot comprehend the work they do (Healers). These roles are no longer about a single 'job' that suits a personality or reflects the work these individuals want to do, it is about fitting an expectation and a need that the role has become. It is not just the police, all professions must be able to cross into other tribal members' skill sets, even when it goes against their core personality traits. Hunters need to document their actions using Gatherer traits; it drives them insane, but it is a necessary evil.

The use of technology and integrated teams means modern businesses lose focus on individuals and instead focus on profit and results. They need a mixed tribe able to cover several roles. Getting the right combination of people willing to provide all the elements needed will determine if the business will be successful. Regardless of the job description, there is no longer a 'fixed' personality trait perfect for completing that role. Many jobs and roles demand most of the elements that the four tribe members possess. Our ever-changing job market demands change, so we mix and match the traits that give us the best possible employee. This is unnatural, but it is now the expected norm. Sometimes, we get it wrong, and those employed in roles cannot meet expectations. Imposer syndrome and fear of being found out push people's buttons, and stress is inevitable.

The skill of managing such a mixed team is so complex that it is almost impossible to ask one person to do it well. Few people can build an effective team from scratch; those who achieve it will do so through luck or experience. People can make a difference to their team by using the information from this part of the book. They can recognise the traits displayed by someone else and change their opinions and management of them.

Listing all the team members' names on a piece of paper and carefully working out their character traits from the CTS can be fun and an easy way to manage a group. To identify why a team is not achieving, look at the make-up. Results will be mixed, but if there are too many people with similar tribal traits, this can be the reason for friction or a lack of action. There needs to be a balance.

Concern	Possible Resolve
Too many tasks are outstanding.	More Protectors are needed.
Paperwork is always late or incorrect.	More Gatherers required
Jobs need to be done more quickly.	Use more Hunters
People feel unsupported or undervalued.	Put more Healers into the team.
Things are not up to standard.	More Protectors and Gatherers required
Low Morale	Add some Healers and Hunters
Lack of direction	Put more Hunters and Protectors in the tribe
Lack of planning	More Healers and Gatherers needed

People in a fully functioning tribe will know and accept each other's personality traits. They do not treat everyone the same; they know which personal strength to use for each differing task. Leaders need to constantly change their communication style, giving each person different amounts of information, all based on the person's personality.

Following simple rules, such as never asking a Gatherer and a Hunter to work together, trying to micromanage a Protector or expecting a Healer to work alone, will benefit the entire tribe.

Never be afraid to change a label. Getting it wrong (think about the 'Nature vs Nurture' element) means we still have three more to try. Experiment with the labels. The effort you put into working out your colleagues, friends, and family members will be paid back in no time, and you will see your daily stress fall away.

Take your time to assess the person; use the tables and charts, and label them. Then, the next time you meet, you will think about their thought process and be able to start reacting positively to their actions rather than getting frustrated because they are not doing it your way.

Being more interactive with people helps. Shaking hands, even if they are longtime friends, helps them open up quicker and allows a more intimate and immediate assessment of their character traits.

Point to note: you cannot shake hands with someone from behind a keyboard. People who email the entire office with important information, believing they are being 'efficient' and 'quick', are missing an important office opportunity. Face-to-face interaction is far more impactful than words on a screen.

THE CAVEMAN PRINCIPLES

PART THREE

12.

MAKING A CHANGE

No one likes making a Change.

Our Caveman ancestors never had to deal with making a personal change. They would never cope in today's world. They were too busy Hunting Mammoths, Gathering firewood, Protecting the tribe and Healing the sick rather than worrying about their weight or making a healthier lifestyle for themselves. The only change they knew was a change in the weather.

They did not comprehend the 'future' and lived in the here and now. They survived every day and knew their purpose in life. Stress was only during and immediately after a fight-or-flight reflex. Humans started from these primitive beginnings. The Caveman grew in skills and knowledge, becoming the dominant creature on this planet. I bet Bert and Errol never knew that any of today's problems would happen.

We deal with so many changes in our lives, adding to them by wanting to make 'life' choices: what to wear, which new career to follow, what to have for lunch... the list is endless. There are changes that we can control and some that we can't.

Life is more complicated now than ever, and getting more complex. Change is not a dirty word; it should be a positive experience. Keeping it in perspective, moving from 'normal' to 'head and shoulders' shampoo is not stressful, but wanting to change jobs to improve your life can be. Moving house should be exciting, but it is also one of the most stressful times we experience. We do not learn from these experiences, as most people move several times in their lifespan. Change can bring stress, especially when a change is forced or creeps upon us.

Making a choice is a skill; without this core function, people become ineffective and stressed. Some modern-day changes are thrust upon us: Food delivered to our door (might be good), being on the verge of self-driving cars (handing over control), and Artificial Intelligence just coming online (massive unknown), all designed in a belief that it will make our lives easier, but there are so many unknown outcomes (we've all seen the Terminator movies). These new computer interactions may be out of our control as they attempt to remove the stress by making choices for us, using the information we have provided through our online presence.

We no longer have a choice to find the deal, handing over our shopping burden to a machine and algorithms. Once we hand this control over to larger corporations, they start to feed in additional needs and wants while taking a larger slice of profits. The feeling may start as liberating, but after reliance on the system, it becomes paralysing when we no longer have a choice, and if we try to step away from using their services, we find ourselves at a complete loss. This is part of the new life as we interact more with computers and AI. Although not the reason for this part of the book, it is important to understand these behaviours. When managing these types of interactions, recognising the situation we place ourselves in is an advantage. There is a lot of work to do, to undo all the damage you may have done, so having a self-serving belief helps. This is mine;

Worrying is not joyful. Don't sweat the stuff that is out of my control. When did worrying change an outcome?

This part of the book is about the changes we want to make to take control of our lives. Making a personal choice and wanting to change ourselves for the better is the desire. This *is* within our control, and this is the opportunity where you can manage your stress. When you make a choice, you need to refocus your thoughts and make the decision more impactful.

In 2019, I had a chance to test this book section in the most extreme change I have ever faced. I had already been through two years of pain and challenges that had broken me before I was medically retired from the police and diagnosed with PTSD, anxiety, and depression. I had no job, was homeless and was single. I was drinking far too much, and I needed to make some real-life changes. I followed my advice and put the work in. Five years later, I am back in charge and happier than ever. I will walk you through my personal route as the change example.

I hope it becomes someone else's survival guide, but the same principles apply even if your change is not this extreme.

The Caveman Change Principles are the same for any change, whether needed, required, or desired. Just pop in your own want/need and follow each step. They will help guide everyone to success. They worked for me, and they will work for you!

Once you have completed the remaining chapters and know the workings of change, we can bring all the Change Principles together, and they will look like this:

- Make a written promise; get the Herder and the Mammoth to agree (more on this to come)
- Describe the desired destination in as much detail as you can.
- Work out how they will both get there, plan, plan and plan.
- Map a route for them to follow and start them off on the right first step of the journey.
- Make sure they both understand that they must cross the line together.
- Use a snapshot image of the desired change.

- Use a Caveman marker to help remind them of the image.
- Manage resistance; check that the company you keep is not holding you back.
- Make sure the journey is broken into shorter manageable chunks; put game-saver milestones in place.
- Celebrate every success.
- Do not keep looking behind you.
- Focus on the destination and stop the Mammoth from getting spooked.

Before starting the steps, you need to understand a few important things. Hunters can skip this part and join us in the next chapter.

We must recognise how to be kind to ourselves. Instead of using 'I want' or 'I need,' rephrase and change the words you tell yourself to something more rewarding, such as "What would I look/feel like if I had..."

Changing how you speak to your inner self will start to make a mental difference in making a change. It takes the sting out of it. When we want to deliver a change message to ourselves, it must hit us in the right place, "I don't want to drink alcohol to excess" is telling our subconscious something different to "What would I feel like in the morning when I stay off alcohol?". Self-communication is vital to how we manage personal change successfully. Invoking emotions and genuinely buying into the change, no matter how easy or challenging the ask is (we will cover this in more detail), will make the difference between success and failure.

Desiring to change something that we do automatically every day is like breaking an addiction. Buying that cake with a coffee, using the lift instead of the stairs, and doing the same job instead of finding a better one needs a different focus and a new way to manage breaking the cycle and making the change. No one wants to give up something we enjoy, but it is the 'why' we want to change. We have little thought of the consequences of our typical daily actions; the cake that makes us fat, unfit and unhealthy is not the culprit. It is how we see it. If we see making a change like breaking an addiction, we can start to understand the process and the work we have to put into it to manage the situation.

Addiction is a dirty, horrid word; no one likes the truth, but acceptance is key. If we want to truly change, we must understand why we do these things and why change is not easy. There are three cycles recognised in addiction, and it works for failure to change as well:

Binge/Intoxication, Withdrawal/Negative affect and Preoccupation/Anticipation.

> Binge/Intoxication, where we do something that gives us joy. An example is the cake with coffee, the following sugar rush, and the pleasure of feeling the melted goo around our mouths as we sit there savouring the sweet hit. Or, in most cases, it has disappeared without us even realising we'd opened the bag.

> Withdrawal/Negative Affect: When we see the empty cupcake case and feel the guilt of eating it in one go and not savouring the taste, we quietly chastise ourselves for having no control and then promise to be more restrained the next time. We start to feel how tight our clothing is getting and then get angry that we cannot control our diets.

Preoccupation/Anticipation comes after a short period of abstinence, but we instinctively grab another muffin when we queue to pay for our Americano, breaking the short-lived promise. Not really wanting that sweet sugar hit, our pre-programmed brains are on autopilot. It is an involuntary action, as we always get a cake when we grab a coffee.

Substituting cake with any other substance or act in the above example will get similar results. Another example is when we fail to do something, and it is the same cycle.

Binge/Intoxication: Not making a spin class you have recently started. You were late from work; something came up, or family issues (insert any excuse here). Instead, you use the extra free hours to relax, watch TV, or do something more fun than sitting in a sweaty spin studio, coming home covered in damp gym kit (we all know about the gym showers; no one wants to use them).

Withdrawal/Negative Affect: The following day, seeing the packed gym bag with clean clothes, you know deep down you had not done something positive that would eventually make you fitter, stronger, and feel better. You promise to make the next session without fail and make a binding promise to work twice as hard the next time.

Preoccupation/Anticipation is when the next session comes up. You remember how relaxing the last evening was when you had extra 'me' time instead of listening to some toned and hyper-excited fitness instructor screaming that you can go up a gear. Deluding yourself, you find an excuse and convince yourself that one more night off will not make a huge difference as you reach for the TV remote.

You can swap the gym scenario for any other excuse for not doing something, such as not looking for a new job, spending time with friends and family, or trying a new hobby or interest.

The cycle is negative, and this is why you fail to make a change in your life. You get caught in a loop, you get frustrated, your stress levels go up, and before you know it, you are stressed because nothing has changed, and you have never moved on from stage one.

It has a compound effect, where several minor hiccups build up, and before you know it, you are asking what the point of trying to make any change is.

Being unable to make change stick and failing to reduce the number of times you push your stress button are significant contributors to this unhealthy negative norm. Managing change is the most challenging area, especially when you look in the mirror and know you need it. Most people prefer to avoid change because it comes with uncertainty. Stressful changes, especially when you work so hard only to fail, will eat you up, and this will recur, ending up in the cycle of starting, tripping and failing. When you think you have mastered a change, you become complacent; before you know it, everything becomes undone, and you are back at the beginning.

When a change is needed, accepting and recognising that it will be disruptive is a must. It takes focus and energy from where you usually need it, making you uncomfortable.

We want 'quick' fixes, but they never work; you need a mindset adjustment to use your energies for the right reasons. We have a finite amount of energy, time and effort. The change that is wanted will require energy, time, and effort. This effort will need to be redirected from another activity. Things to contemplate;

- Do you live to work, or do you work to live? Spending eight to ten hours a day, five days a week, at a job is essential for paying our bills, but you must make the balance of effort count for something important to you. Much of our adult life is spent doing what someone else tells us to do. It is 'just a job' but does it fulfil you?

- No matter what you do for a living, it is still only a job. Jobs can and do change. You work to get paid, and the rest is up to you. No one wants to drag work worries home. Spending your free time grumbling and complaining is a waste of energy.

- When I was a cop, I had to do something to break my mental state. My work boots stayed in my locker at the end of my shift. They never came home with me. This signified that the boots and my work worries stayed away from my home.

THE CAVEMAN PRINCIPLES

- Without good employees, there will be no business.
- You are important in your workplace, regardless of what your line manager thinks. Your work may have all the control, but you have the power to make a customer happy and make a difference. Without your professionalism, experience, qualifications and drive, your company would not be as successful as it is. People want to feel appreciated and valued for their work. Research suggests that a lack of recognition determines why employees change jobs.
- They may pay you for your time and deserve your focus and energy, but they must treat you with respect and give recognition. We all want different things, but thanking and rewarding someone is a common need and incredibly powerful. You can change your focus; only you will know if you have more to give and, more importantly, where you want to put that energy, especially if it is
- a thankless job, so consider your options.
- Be under no illusions. If you leave a job to try a new challenge, don't let your ego believe you cannot be replaced.

- Switching your focus from the challenge of a change to a result makes it easier to accept and gives us a higher chance of success.
- No matter what the change is, whether losing a few pounds, stopping drinking, or starting a new career, you must focus on the outcome you desire, not the here and now, which you already know and live. Knowing you aim for a change creates momentum and helps you achieve the desired result.
- What control do you have over Change?
- Some changes are not in your control. There is no point in fighting an imposed change (think illness), especially when acceptance can be more beneficial. However, when lifestyle choices are essential, you must choose to change. You will reduce resistance, stop stress, and free up energy when you own it.
- As an extreme example, people who are diagnosed with severe health conditions, diabetes, heart concerns and other severe conditions shouldn't worry about the healthier choices of food that they must eat. Instead, shifting focus to wanting to

feel good and prolonging life makes any change more palatable.
- If you are being made redundant, you have no control. However, you do have control over what you do next. You can put the energy from worrying into what job you want to do next. There will be stress, but taking control of opportunities to retrain, reconnect, and try something new is a far better use of that energy.
- You have the power of change in your hands. Freeing energy for your mind and heart requires realigning your thought process. If you are serious about making a change, change your thought process.

Change needs to be appealing. You must find the right reason for you. It must make you want to change, not cause you to fear and resist it. Making change more appetising means grabbing your emotional thoughts, not focusing on your rational brain.

You must not concentrate on a situation's negative aspects or how it will affect you. Worrying will not help anyone in this situation. You should only focus on the ability to move forward. Finding the more appealing parts of change and a way to support that dream is far better and less damaging. This is far less stressful than pointless worrying and being stuck, unable to do anything.

Harking back to our Caveman ancestors, they had a simple choice: make a change or die. They could either stay in a cave that was flooding because it was their home, or get out and find a new, drier one. Their change process was more straightforward because there was little choice. Their simpler lifestyles seem ideal compared to our current living standards. They were free with no mortgage or schooling boundaries for their cave kids. Your options might seem more complex in today's standard of living, but strip it down to the essentials, and the results remain the same.

Thanks to social media, we live in a society where everyone knows everything, regardless of their training or experience. We have to contend with others who give an unchecked, loud and vocal opinion. Social Media can dictate how we live, telling governments what they should do. The Fear of Missing Out (FOMO) is real. This is what I call letting your emotional Mammoth off the lead.

THE CAVEMAN PRINCIPLES

We don't worry about catching it with a "Not our problem until it becomes our problem" attitude. My suggestion is to cut out following any trends on the internet, stop taking advice from strangers popping up in your feed and work a few things out for yourself.

When people make a change, rumours and gossip thrive. Cast your mind back to when someone you know tried to do some exercise or make a positive change in their life. Have you supported them, made fun behind their backs, and belittled their progress? You know from experience that our friends and family are not as supportive as you'd like them to be, probably because you have tried the same things a few times before and got nowhere. Please don't give up. We will work on that later in the book.

Reading all this, you'd be forgiven for thinking, "What's the point?" Well, facing the truth and putting change into perspective is good to acknowledge. Hard work is the recognition part; it is better than ignorance and failure. As we work through the principles, you will see the pitfalls of your previous attempts, and then, with the knowledge, you can plan to avoid them. Changing how you tell people why you want to change and asking for their active support will help; we are back to talking and communicating again. Reducing stress and stopping yourself from hitting the button while having the support you need to make a positive change is the dream.

The challenge is to take control of your change Mammoth and guide it through the trips, hazards, and pitfalls of change. Using the Caveman Change Principles is about personal reflection. Digging deeper into your psyche will get uncomfortable, but you will have to break a few eggs to make this omelette.

You want to improve your life, health, and wealth, so what is stopping you? Whether a change is stressful or fun is in the eye of the person who understands why, when, what, and how. Change is a positive advancement, not a scary blocker to a better life.

Those who start without acknowledging a few things will fail because they fail to understand the complex nature of change.

Never fear change, as without it, we would all still be living in a cave, and Apple would be something that only grew on trees. We would never have invented televisions; the big Friday night show would be Errol showing us his badly drawn picture of a Mammoth on the cave wall.

You will learn the art of internal communication, switching focus from the current tiresome process, such as eating cabbage, to using the emotional draw of not having a beer gut over the top of your trousers, making your change successful and easier. Walking through the Caveman Change Principles together, you will see why people fail. I will show you a route to change that you may have never seen before. Understanding the 'why' and 'how' of change might even unlock a few new ideas inside you. Committing to change using the Caveman Change Principles will make your life easier and less stressful.

13.

THE CAVEMAN HERDER AND THE PET MAMMOTH

The right and left sides of the brain – Fact or Fiction?

The Caveman Principles are about keeping things simple; no medical jargon or complex psychology studies are repeated here. It is a simple way to help explain how the soft, squishy stuff in our nogging works. Helping to explain is the Caveman Herder and his pet Mammoth.

Imagine what it would be like to control your desires and wishes in your day-to-day life. It would make a real impact. The new outlook will be success, acceptance of differing results, and focus on positive outcomes. The benefit will be reducing the daily, self-sabotaging button presses you endure when you force change and see no results. Instead, you can start to enjoy the new changes you make for yourself.

THE CAVEMAN PRINCIPLES

It must always be fun to make any change work and, more importantly, stay as a new habit. If the process and the outcome were achieved through slogging and beasting your subconscious, there is a huge chance you will fail to make any impact. If you miraculously reach your destination, chances are that all that hard work will come undone as soon as you stop focusing on the goal.

Using the Caveman Change Principles makes things more manageable. They turn the slog into smiles, the hard work into excitement. The principles use a similar thought process to the head and heart theory. Changing your mind about how you view and manage change means that from now on, there will be a Caveman Herder (the head) and a pet Mammoth (the heart).

To set the record straight, your head and heart are the same thoughts in your brain. They are thought processes only differentiated as emotional thought (Mammoth), how you feel at that moment and the rational thought of what you must do (Herder).

Psychologists once believed that there were two sides to the brain, the left and right hemispheres working independently from each other rather than as one big organ. Although some of this may have been debunked with the latest brain scanning equipment, it fits with our narrative, and as this thing fits into the cavity of our noodle, we have to try to make sense of it. The brain is split down the middle, connected with nerves and links that a supercomputer could never copy. Using the old theory of the split, the Caveman Change principles will pick up a similar vein.

The typical left side of our brain (Herder) has long been believed to be our logical, analytical side, where all the planning is done, the 'Thinking' side of the brain. This is the side where our instincts and rational thoughts reside.

Your Herder likes to try to make sense of the world around us. With fast analytical thinking, the Herder can get you out of trouble. The Herder looks at all the information available and can make a split-second, reasoned, rational decision based on it. The Herder rules the roost; it likes fast decision-making and does not debate or make exceptions. Once a decision is made, it passes off the actual doing part to other parts of the brain.

The Herder has a fantastic talent for jumping to conclusions and barrelling into situations, jumping in with both feet and wanting to change direction halfway through a process. Regardless of your character in the CTS, this Herder identifies with a Hunter. Imagine a tiny Hunter's conscience sitting on your shoulder, telling you what to do, wanting you to act impulsively and not think about the consequences. The Herder looks after all the tricky and boring stuff processed in our heads, like language functions, reading, writing, and the ability to speak. Herders are the ones who interpret the literal meaning of a complex conversation (2+2 = might be 5).

Opposite to the typical right side of the brain (the Mammoth's side), this is where you do your intuitive and emotional bits, also known as the 'Doer' side, or the emotional Healer character of sorts. This is where the grunt work is managed. After the Herder has concluded its work, completing the task is the Mammoth's problem.

The Mammoth looks after everything concerning emotions, including loving, hating, enjoying, and fearing things.

THE CAVEMAN PRINCIPLES

Unlike the Herder, your Mammoth has a much slower thinking response and cannot appreciate fast-paced decisions. It hates fast changes and needs time to adjust, which is the opposite of the Herder's thoughts.

The Mammoth likes boring. It gets comfortable in a rut, enjoying repetition and getting easy, cheap rewards. It is your Mammoth that becomes addicted to the wrong things, such as alcohol, caffeine, sugar, gambling or being sat on the sofa. The Mammoth is a giant lazy creature of habit, and it takes vast amounts of effort to do anything new or get it to do anything different. Getting it to want to do anything else is very difficult when it gets caught in a rut. The Mammoth is also very skittish, scared of its shadow, and needs to be treated with care.

Slightly off-topic, but important to understand that phobias are part of the Mammoth's domain; they are collected like medals. The Mammoth is a complete coward. It does not tackle any issue; instead, it allows them to fester in the corner, not brave enough to tackle the source of the problem.

Phobias manifest when someone has either been taught or experienced a terrifying ordeal. As a child, I could climb ladders; they were great fun. One was left at the side of our family house by the window cleaner, and I managed to get to the very top of the ladder, looking around without fear.

Then I got caught by my mother. She was screaming, with true panic in her voice. When I returned to ground level, she scolded me for doing something incredibly dangerous. To add to the impact, when I had forgotten all about being up the ladder, my father scolded me when he returned from work. The knowledge of being caught, the induced panic, and the pain and embarrassment of doing something fun have culminated in a fear that I still feel when I see a ladder today; it all came from this experience.

Putting it into practice, the Mammoth linked both the scoldings about the ladder and bang. I had an irrational fear of ladders. This fear of being caught doing something my mother thought I should not have done meant my Mammoth had not allowed me to be more than six feet off the ground on any ladder before my knees started to knock. This is how the Mammoth records, links and uses experiences to make you form an opinion. Although my Mammoth still gets scared using a ladder, using my change theory, it is no longer a massive phobia, and I can clean my upstairs windows. You can use these principles to manage phobias; finding the phobia's cause will make it much easier to accomplish.

Back to how you can make a change, the Caveman Herder and the Mammoth are opposite characters, pulling in differing directions of change, but both wanting to make a difference. To make real progress, they must agree to work together, choose the path, and make it a lasting habit.

Using my scenario back in 2019, I had a choice: After 19 years of wearing a uniform, my Mammoth could not comprehend doing anything else. I could either lose myself in pity, as everything I once loved, cherished, and thought precious and worthy was gone, or I could rebuild a life worth living. My lifeline was that I knew the entire content of the first edition of this book, so I had no excuse for not being able to make things work.

Handing in my uniform and my warrant card ripped off a chunk of my soul, which my Mammoth had clung to for all those years and was unwilling to give up. Stuck in a rut, it needed to be looked after. Self-care is not what you think; instead, it is more Mammoth-care.

I made a list of the most important issues and marked which ones I could cope with, manage, and achieve. I took time to allow my Mammoth to adjust and realise it had to make the journey with me, then got to work on rebuilding. I planned in as much detail as possible about how I would do it, plotted a route for how it would be achieved, and learned how to keep the Herder from ruining the progress and work. I wanted to be in a stronger, better position than I had ever been; at the time, that was harder to convince myself than I thought. I could picture myself where I wanted to be, and I used my old dog tag in my pocket as my marker to help remind myself of where I wanted to be. I broke contact with all my old work colleagues, which would make my mammoth lose focus, and I made sure I knew what my milestone successes looked like.

For every recognisable success, I celebrated it. I went out for dinner, spent days out, bought myself a car, and went on holiday.

When I wanted to check how far I had come, I stopped myself and instead focused on the next celebration milestone. None of this was an overnight success, and it took dedication.

In five short years, I have become a successful Innovation Project Manager, managing multi-million-pound projects. I am paid well and regularly praised. I have bought, completely renovated, and now live in a beautiful home. I am debt-free and have a wonderful wife and a fantastic life. My drinking is well under control, and I have circled back to re-editing this book and restarting my writing career and speaker business.

Without the ability to stop my Mammoth from getting spooked, controlling my narrative, and pushing forward, I can guarantee that I would be in a deep hole full of self-pity.

Hopefully, you can see many of my challenges and how many pitfalls a new desired change could have fallen into. If you don't tackle change properly, it will fail. If you insert anything other than my example for your desired change, such as wanting to have a new weight training regime, signing up for a gym, losing weight, or even changing your job, then you can get the same result by following the rules.

Nothing is forced when the Herder and the pet Mammoth agree, and it makes things happen. The Caveman Change Principles can get them talking, agreeing, and progressing in any of these circumstances. You need to revolutionise how you tackle change. If you can get them both to want to change, then rather than just a one-off visit to a new shop, gym or a single CV submission, you can make it your new routine and celebrate the results. You can make it exciting and fun.

If you need one more thought to ponder, consider why so many New Year's resolutions fail. Spoiler alert: they only involve the Herder making the choice. The quick decision of 'oh, I forgot to think of one', rushing to a conclusion, leaves the Mammoth out of the plan. Doing this makes it angry and scared, which means any change has zero chance of success. Using the Caveman Change principles, you need a plan. A new map, a new route and a new destination which must be managed without freaking out the Mammoth. Simplicity is the key, and you cannot skip the effort that will be required every day. Please give it some Mammoth-care; engage both the Herder and the Mammoth. We will get the Herder and the Mammoth on the new path together; it will be challenging, but not impossible. Things are easier when they start the journey together; don't let them jump off early before considering all the consequences.

Taking your time and putting in the effort will prevent the Herder from dragging the Mammoth to the gym. The result will be a failure. As far as the Mammoth is concerned, it is comfortable sitting on the sofa every night. This is what it is used to doing. It might be convinced to put itself out for a single visit to a gym, believing it is a waste of time and even thinking it will get a beach body if they do it once. One visit will not be enough, but the Mammoth has not been told this. Once it has been, the Herder will push to go again, but the Mammoth is unconvinced. The Herder will run out of energy or willpower to keep pushing and realise there is no point.

The missed first step is the plan, research, and showing a strong reason to get the Mammoth into the gym, getting it to buy into the change before the Herder jumps in with both feet will upset the apple cart.

Mammoths are not the only problem. The Herder has their part to play as they call all the initial shots, not thinking things through, only seeing the logical reason for the change and ignoring the emotional pull. They need to slow down and start to think about the impact on the Mammoth. Herders can make instant decisions for what they perceive to be immediate needs, like signing up for a gym, but they have no stamina for long-term change. Herders get very excited and have difficulty containing their new buzz, becoming loud and the only voice of reason in your head. Their impatient, demanding nature wants us to try new things, not thinking of the long-term consequences. It means that our outlook is only a flash of brilliance. If you continually listen to them, you have a new flash every night, quickly forgetting the original decision you wanted. Your Mammoth cannot keep up, gets no momentum and loses interest.

The skill is slowing your Herder and getting the pet Mammoth into a position where it can start

THE CAVEMAN PRINCIPLES

to change its opinion. Give it time to prepare and come to terms with this new idea and its meaning. The Mammoth thrives on learnt behaviour; it can be compared to turning an oil tanker, which takes time, room, and patience.

Suppose you get a Mammoth to start walking a new path. In that case, it means stopping visiting the sofa after work and doing nothing but watching television, replacing it with an exciting new interest. But if you do anything it does not like or expect, it will return to its old habits. Habits need to be broken; Mammoths must be shown that there is a better path, making them want to make a behavioural change, not just a physical one.

Failure occurs when you listen to your herder, pack your gym bag, and sign up for a year's membership at the local sweatbox. The momentum and wants of the Herder override the Mammoth's wants, forcing it off the comfortable sofa and into a noisy building where you beast yourself until you can no longer stand and want to throw up. The Herder loves this, but the Mammoth has already decided it is not willing to swap out the sofa.

The Mammoth does not understand why you are doing this and does not see it as fun. It just wants to return to that comfortable rut on the sofa and never return to the mirror reflecting admiring crowd building. It fails to understand why it is there.

Your Herder loses interest quickly as they are not the Mammoth motivator. It has no patience, wanting the Mammoth to see things as they do. Why can't it see why this change is needed? Does it not know you are tied into a contract? What the Herder fails to realise is that the weight and momentum of the Mammoth is what is needed to make the change happen. Herders want the Mammoth to feel the same excitement and use the logical thinking that they have. The Mammoth is uninterested and does not see the reason for the change, as you have failed to get the Mammoth to feel the reason or the benefit. It does not feel it is in a safe space and will not be interested in doing something it does not feel is worth it. With no emotional pull, all effort is lost. No matter how logical the Herder thinks it is, you have missed the real need for the change.

You need to access and touch the Mammoth's emotions. It is easier than you think. You must first forget the use of logic. The Herder can handle logic; it already uses it every day. You are missing convincing thoughts on why the change is needed. You must concentrate on motivating the Mammoth, hitting its heartstrings.

Quieting the Herder helps. Acknowledge the thoughts, but let them sit for a while. It will be great not to let it react and race ahead. Take your time. Start by understanding that the Herder and the Mammoth must walk the new path together.

When they finally get on the same path, finding an emotional reason that the Mammoth understands is key, but you must not relax. There is still work to do. The early part is easy. The Mammoth needs to be led and has to feel safe. If it gets stressed, it will run, returning to the last comfortable rut that it understands and can manage. If that is the sofa, you risk starting at the beginning, so put in some game-saving milestones and not all the effort is lost.

The time spent convincing the Mammoth that a change is needed is well spent. It must be an authentic emotional tug. Mine was survive or thrive.

There are several ways to do this; spending time on finding your motivation is key. Remember that one size does not fit all. Try different combinations, then use combinations from your list, the strongest ones that balance the Mammoths' and Herders' needs. These are your thoughts, not someone else's. It only needs to resonate with your thoughts and beliefs.

Make lists, dream, manifest, and cover all the emotions you will feel during and after the change. To-do lists and reasoning have their place, but will not help here. If you want change to happen, it must be of real emotional benefit and making the Mammoth believe it is possible is the key. Using all emotions is necessary; linking being happy, loving, fun, pain-free, active, and having focused outcomes is needed. Try different ways to access your Mammoth, use photos, wish boards, notes, do whatever you need, and suggest changes that will hit the Mammoth right in the gut. Do not pull any punches. Make it take notice.

My choice was painful and needed hours of inner thought and reflection. If I were to write my entire plan, it would need another book. All the detail was held in my head and on a few pieces of paper, which helped me work bits out, but to highlight my journey, I focused on being stable, free of PTSD triggers, and not needing alcohol to manage my headspace. Everything else, such as my job, love life and business, fell into that plan as I worked through it.

It needed to be such a strong emotional hit, right in the sweet spot, for the feeling to land the full impact of why my change was necessary. The best pressure points are using family, especially our kids. Mammoths love our kids and will accept change if it means thinking about them. My son was a huge reason to pull through this low part of my life. Unless he reads this book, he will have no reason to think he had anything to do with my transformation; the last thing you should do is tell them and put unnecessary pressure on them to manage your change.

If you get it right, your Mammoth will not need to be convinced about protecting others. They can make instant changes, especially when it comes to loved ones. This emotional weakness can be exploited to force the Mammoth to accept a change and get things moving.

The problem is getting the Herder to accept the responsibility of carrying out their initial decision and not passing it off. If the Herder does not start playing the long game, they risk ruining an opportunity and the Mammoth stopping, even turning back the way it came, or worse, running off into the brush.

The Mammoth is a three-ton beast which the Herder cannot move alone. It takes a lot of effort to do anything, so for a Mammoth to exert that energy, it needs to believe it is for a worthwhile cause. Remember, the Mammoth is lazy and skittish; using loud, angry shouts and noises will not work. The Mammoth would love a quick win, as long as it does not ruin its learnt habits and behaviours, the Herder can carry on as long as it does not have to do anything. When it is moving, you must watch out for shortcuts and any stupid ideas the Herder has. The only option is to convince a Mammoth to do something positive, which takes time and effort, needs a plan and a map to follow, is emotionally charged and has plenty of stops along the way.

Using the Herder's willpower never works. Full of motivation, the Herder starts enthusiastically, wanting to stride off down the new path, leaving the Mammoth behind, as they believe this is the easiest option. They are not interested in wasting time talking about all their feelings and do not want to involve the Mammoth. When they realise they need the Mammoth, they grab hold of it and put all their effort into pushing it out the door. The Herder shoves the Mammoth down the new path, using every bit of strength.

The Herder shoves and pushes it as far up the path as they can manage. Just like willpower, the Herder will run out of energy, ending up exhausted. The Mammoth is no longer being pushed; it feels nervous and must start thinking for itself. It has no idea what to do. The reason was not explained. It feels lost, and panic sets in. The Mammoth does exactly what it wants to do; it goes back to what feels normal in its comfortable surroundings and runs back into its familiar rut.

For any successful change, there must be a common goal. The Herder and the Mammoth must understand what it means, combining the logical head and the emotional heart. This must be achieved before you allow them to journey through a change. The Mammoth is both proud and scared. Convincing it that the change is worthwhile before it is out of its comfort zone and into the unknown on a potentially dangerous path works in your favour.

The Mammoth cannot be blamed when it has been shown and has committed to the original change; it knows the plan and is emotionally linked to the new route. If the route suddenly changes, then how is it going to understand how this new route is going to improve its life? Unlike the Herder, the Mammoth needs time to understand why a route change is needed. It must stick to the plan, or it will start to doubt and think about returning to its old ways.

Herders need to be taught the important job of watching the Mammoth. Even when they commit, Mammoths are happy to do something 'one last time'. They will try to slip past the Herder for that 'one last cigarette' and use the old 'I'll start tomorrow' or the 'one won't hurt' tricks. Once emotionally charged, the Herder must constantly remind the Mammoth why it is on the new path and not to return to the old comfortable path by allowing it to light up that cigarette or get back on the sofa when it should be going to the gym. The Herder's effort is best served by watching the Mammoth and guiding it back using emotional pulls rather than the willpower of pushing and shoving.

Herders love making instant changes and always want to try the new route marked 'shortcut'; these are change traps. Set up like honeytraps, they will scupper any effort. They could be social media influencers or marketing gurus promising quicker results. Should their marketing make you change your plan, the Mammoth will get spooked, as you have not consistently followed your agreed-upon plan, so stick to the agreed-upon route. If you want to be agile and change the plan, plan to change the plan and engage your Mammoth first.

Change traps get your Herder very excited. Take time, take stock, and consider the emotional impact this will have. The Herder sees they get all the benefits of the change without doing more than necessary, wanting the new routine to shorten the agreed journey and reach the destination faster. It can even dump the emotional Mammoth sooner without dealing with all the problematic stuff.

It might be a simple change from a regular day of going to the gym or a new healthy snack with a shinier label or funnier shape than the last one; it might even be a new job recruiter or hobby. Whatever it might be, if not consulted, the Mammoth will not like it when it is not emotionally involved. It gets stuck, not wanting to change the route or continue down the one it has agreed to be on.

Even the smallest element of change after the Mammoth has committed to a new path has the potential to spook it, and it will take the option to run away, not only ensuring the change has failed but also making it harder to retrace any of the steps. Life happens; life can get in the way. The trick is to recognise when your Herder loses focus on the route. When they get distracted, quickly returning them to where they left off can save things from becoming a complete failure.

When I was not getting interviews for the Project Manager role I wanted, I considered becoming a delivery driver. Seeing job adverts, I was willing to go for the easier option (a shortcut) rather than stick to the agreed route I had planned. As much as I wanted to give up, I spent time, did some Mammoth care, got my Herder to check on the Mammoth's welfare, and allowed myself to reconcile and work things out.

I realised things were still achievable, feeling reassured, and, with some reflection and effort, I re-jigged my CV and had an interview the following week, starting a new position a few weeks after that. Change is a long slog. If we fail to prepare, we prepare to fail, which fits perfectly (thanks, Benjamin Franklin). Expecting to hit a few bumps on the path will take the edge off and prepare you to manage when you do, and not have to change the outcome.

14.
PLAN THE ROUTE

Have a clear strategy.

Change is hard; otherwise, you wouldn't need this book. You have to be committed. Going through a change needs planning; treat it like you are going on a journey to a new and exotic location. You do not just rock up. You do some research. What do you need to pack? Do you need jabs? What currency do they use? What language do they speak? The most important thing is how you are going to get there. There are so many important questions, and like making a change, you are going to want to plan the journey.

The change journey needs the Herder and the Mammoth to go on it together, in complete unison. The Herder's logical thoughts, against an emotionally charged Mammoth temperament, means the route must be balanced. There are two stages of change planning: showing the Mammoth what is involved by mapping it all out and engaging its emotions. Herders like planning, but must be forced to add more emotional detail.

You may want to make a change to make your life better, but for me, everything had been ripped away, and I was starting from scratch. Whether you wish to improve a small part of your life or have to make a complete do-over, it needs time, focus and dedication. It is the most important part of the change. I initially took a lot of time to decide what to focus on. I realised I wanted to be secure, paid well and live a good life. These were the bare bones, but they were my starting point. Then, as the picture started to develop, I was able to flesh out the rest as I began to make more decisions. I started to picture myself standing in my home, seeing money in my bank account and enjoying my work. The plan then started to shape how I would get there. My first dilemma was work; I needed an income. I was interested in Project Management and thought I would be good at it. I needed training and spoke to loads of people in Social Media groups. I got loads of advice and started my journey. I planned to get into project management at any level and grow my experience. Crafting a CV was part of the plan, and knowing how to get it out into the world and what company I was prepared to work for. The route and journey kept growing with more and more detail being added, such as which job sites I would use.

The plan was my route and my map to the destination, and it did not stop at getting the job. I had plans that ran alongside the job hunt and ones that extended from it. It was carefully crafted and as much detail as I could add.

Next was convincing my Mammoth that change was needed. I looked at all the route steps, thought about it some more, and knew I could follow them. My motivation and my Mammoth stirred, and this was when I hit it with emotional punches. How good would I feel to get my CV out there? How happy would I be when I get an interview, a job offer, and even when I start to work? My big picture was as loud and as brightly painted as I could make it. I used every positive emotion to get my Mammoth moving; joy, hope, gratitude, interest, and fun levels were all used. I felt these emotions when I asked questions, such as how I would feel when offered an interview. These formed part of the journey and gave my Mammoth something to look forward to and motivation to keep it going.

I asked and answered my questions, writing them down to add to the journey. They came in handy when I hit a few potholes, such as when I found I needed help with my CV and realised my mistakes, which were quickly rectified. It was just a tiny bump, and as I had thought about the problem of my CV not tracking well, the journey was not derailed. I had tolerate, transfer, treat, terminate or take the risk next to each potential pothole. If these concerns were in my control, I could manage them, but for those that were not, I changed the situation instead. If I had no control, I would not worry about them until it became a problem.

Thinking about how your Mammoth might react throughout the planning process, you can pre-empt the pitfalls, making those parts of the journey more fun and exciting, or accept the risk and move on. You must convince the Herder to stay on track, stick to the plan, and not let them wander, which they will always want to do. I know how hard it is, as when I was not getting any interviews, my Herder started to offer more job ideas, and I almost went off track. Holding out, I researched the state of Project manager recruitment and saw that everyone was struggling, not just me. A few weeks later, I landed the perfect job as an assistant project manager at UKRI. Managing both sides is challenging; it will fail if you don't keep them both on track.

From the first thought about wanting to change something, you must stop and plan it before taking the plunge. Writing down a thought-out process in chronological order hits your Herder's sweet spot; create a solid plan. Your Mammoth will want to watch it unfold and will become interested. Once the plan has been written, sign and date it. Buy a cheap glass frame and frame it. Using your original notes, rough scribbles, cross-outs, and unchecked spelling documents will work best. A polished and well-put-together piece of paper looks too clinical and will not inspire. You need the Mammoth to feel that the work you have put into it, the more organic and emotional you keep it, the more motivational it will be. When framed, put it somewhere where it will be seen and checked, and use it as a daily reminder of your change commitment; mine was on my desk next to my laptop. This helped both my Herder and Mammoth to stay on track.

You want to follow the designated route. Take your time. You want to get the Mammoth desensitised to the idea of change and not scare it by dropping the whole idea out of nowhere. Show the beast that you are committed, and the effort will not be wasted. There is a plan, and it will be followed.

Self-reflection to identify potential pitfalls will help manage blockers. Mine were my old work colleagues. They kept me in a world I could no longer be part of and pulled my focus away from being someone else. Being honest with yourself is difficult and even impossible at times. You do not have to share your inner thoughts; they can stay private.

Questions that might kick-start identifying your pitholes: If you wish to lose weight, ask yourself if bullies caused an eating habit or if it was because of having your kids, and it was easier to snack. Was the smoking addiction caused by watching parents smoke, or the caffeine doses caused by copying people at work? There might be obvious triggers that can release the Mammoth from its rut. You will need time and be willing to take a good look inward. Finding a trigger can be hard, but it can also catapult the progress of change forward, making it less challenging.

You should never demand action to clarify your plan; instead, make a statement. Make it a reasonable request, include the wording of the change required and add what you want to happen. A final desired change you strive to achieve makes all the difference.

- to give up smoking *forever*
- to be able to run five miles non-stop, *with ease*
- to lose two stone and *maintain it*
- to get a new job and *enjoy it*
- to stop gambling and *save £1,000*
- to fit in a pair of 36-inch jeans *comfortably*
- to stop abusing alcohol and *moderate it*

Declaring a desired statement will determine the end goal. Make it refined and clear. Your Herder and Mammoth can only work together with a clear and defined path.

Attempting to use an instruction gives a negative feel and causes resistance. Everybody hates being denied or told what to do, so why do it to yourself? It does not work. A plan should **not** start with an "I will not…"

- I will not *eat any more chocolate*
- I will not *smoke any more cigarettes*
- I will not *complain about my job*

After you try telling yourselves not to do anything for a long period, you ignore the 'not' in the demand, which no longer works.

Writing and telling yourselves, "I will not chew my fingernails," is dangerous. A more positive instruction, like "I will grow my fingernails," makes a better impact. A Mammoth or Herder cannot ignore or change the intent of such a desired outcome.

Adding reasons to the change will maximise the intent and engage the Mammoth. To give up smoking forever, consider adding the emotional and physical impact, and it will make the change feel fuller:

- so that I can breathe better and be healthier
- so that I smell fresh and sweeter
- so that I have a longer life with my family
- so that I can afford nicer things
- so that I will have more money in the bank
- so that I no longer have to endure the sound of rolling eyes when I say I am popping outside

The more emotional you can make these, the more impactful the reason becomes. The more personal you make them, the more reason you have to do it. If people comment on the smell, adding their name, especially if it is a close family member, is incredibly impactful.

Finding a reason for change can come from anywhere. Observation and conversations are great places to start, either by you or another person. If you feel brave, ask others, but be prepared for some honest truths you may have to deal with. Being told that you smell like an ashtray or being the joke about buttons firing off a shirt can be brutal, but impactful. You know you have a strong reason to start a change if it hits a nerve.

START DATE

Mammoths love procrastination. Get your diary out right now, open your phone app, and make an entry for today. Make your commitment, and start your change statement. Start the journey, put this book down for a minute and do it; delaying will allow the Mammoth to wriggle past the commitment and back to its comfortable rut. Get the basics started and done, and then the rest gets easier.

Research some simple facts; they can add emotional weight to your change. Dr. Google and Prof. Reddit are great at providing details you may never have considered.

- What are the risks for someone who is obese?
- What does abusing alcohol do to the body?
- What foods can improve skin conditions?
- Tell me a weight loss story
- Where does my money go when I gamble?
- What are the risks of second-hand smoke?
- What do earthworms eat? (This is just an interesting question and possibly not change-related, but I like the term detritivores.)

Your Mammoth likes emotional detail. It will become more interested when it sees what you have planned and knows it will experience an emotional response. New information is always good; learning important facts can emotionally charge your Mammoth and make the effort worthwhile.

Mammoths are easier to move when a plan comes together. Start mapping it out using all the information. The Mammoth will realise that this change has a different feel. Your Herder is not about to shove it around; it can make its mind up, and with this fresh approach, it gives the Mammoth confidence to move by itself. Suddenly, the Herder can do their job and guide, keeping the momentum going and conserving their energy for the path ahead. It does not matter what change you want to make happen. The principles are all the same. Whether you are looking for a new job, getting fitter, stopping smoking, losing weight, or making more family time, if you make a change plan, don't short-change the work needed.

Once the plan is drawn, signed and sealed, your Herder must team up with the Mammoth and agree on how they will add more detail to the journey. The map is the critical route, a set of instructions that, when followed, will guarantee change. Adding detail is good, but changing the route is not.

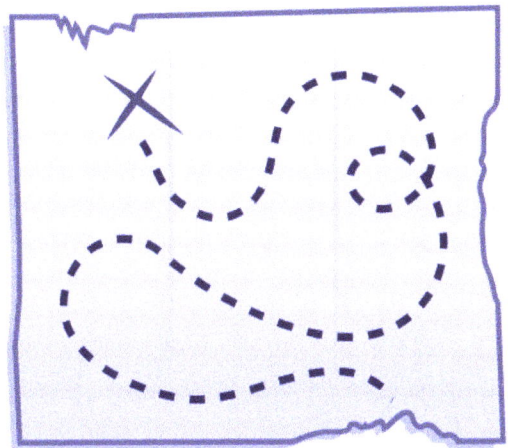

As with any map, it is easier to start at the beginning. Plot along the course of the map on how you will reach the end, adding when you will stop, rest, and reflect and for how long. If you know of any foreseen traps, such as upcoming parties (smokers and drinkers), events or triggers, plan to manage them and unsubscribe from emails that will tempt you. You need to be prepared and know how you will tackle them. Keeping a diary will keep you on track; adding your thoughts, feelings, successes, and failures will get them out of your head. Using technology, adding daily voice notes or messages helps clear your mind. Setting reminders on your calendar app is easy; you never go out without it. This is an easy win unless your change is to be less phone-reliant.

Prepare yourself. The journey will be long, and at times, it will get tough. If change were easy, you wouldn't need this book. Having as many tools and options as possible would be beneficial, but remember to stick to the plan and keep moving toward the goal.

Synchronising the Herder and Mammoth gets easier as you map, keep a clear path and put dates, times, and even locations where you need to fix the route. If you can get into a routine, a new comfy Mammoth rut will appear, and your change map will become easier to follow.

The Herder will know when a breakthrough happens before the Mammoth, so manage your milestones so you do not lose one of them; more on this later.

The Mammoth must stay focused and constantly be reminded that there is a route to follow in the planned journey ahead. Poking emotions and refreshing the memory for the reasons will keep it pushing forward. Constantly showing the Mammoth this level of detail will keep it motivated. You do not want it to feel lost, get frightened, and lose the path. Knowledge and planning will keep the Mammoth calm. There can be no big surprises, no change of direction or distraction. You want it to be as relaxed as it can be.

Mammoths are also forgetful; this is why you need reminders. A calendar entry of your change, your reasons written out and easily accessible, printed, scribbled out and placed somewhere you must look at every day (mirrors and inside the kitchen cupboard doors are good places). The Mammoth appreciates knowing where it is starting from and, even more, a reminder of where it is going and what emotions it will experience. Being forgetful, if it is not poked and reminded regularly, it will find an easier path to follow and will be happy to follow it back to the beginning.

THE CAVEMAN PRINCIPLES

A massive pitfall to avoid is deciding to change direction because of circumstances, choice, or it being imposed on you. You must do everything to prevent this, but if you have to, you must plan a short detour. Update your map and plan, and let the Mammoth understand it. Like any slow, anxious, scared animal, it needs time to adjust, so changes in the route must be handled delicately and carefully.

When the Mammoth forgets, the Herder is distracted and excited about other avenues. Herders must also be reminded of the agreed route and their role in motivating the Mammoth; they are not allowed to wander off. The herders may believe they have found a better route and want to make quick changes. The only route that was carefully planned was the one they had to follow, regardless of their supposed findings. Make them stick to the agreed plan, and if you need to rethink things, put a milestone check in your diary far in advance, up to five or six months away, and only when you get there, change it. This gives the Mammoth time to digest, adjust, and know it is coming.

The hardest battle is helping the Herder and the Mammoth understand that change takes time and is not an overnight success. The more detail you add, the better the Mammoth's chance of making it a reality.

Changing anything in the plan, even if it is a regular time slot, a day, or an activity, will give the Mammoth wriggle room. This explains when a regular gym goer finds it hard to keep going if classes get cancelled, weight machines are under repair or being updated; these little changes throw the Mammoth off balance, and all the momentum is lost. If you must change, make sure you get back to the old plan as quickly as possible. Do not let the Herder find a new route and allow them to open any excuse the Mammoth can use.

To help motivate, pop a tick or an entry against your diary appointment after every successful event. Showing proof of ongoing success will encourage and inspire both Herder and Mammoth to keep going. When you stop at a milestone, you can check progress. They will see a chain of unbroken attendance and successes, which will make them more committed and make it harder for them to want to stop.

Each completed appointment brings you closer to the goal and your desired outcome. The path of change becomes a habit, and as the Mammoth likes 'habits,' these are the comfortable ruts in which you want it to live.

Working a typical Monday-to-Friday nine-to-five job is more straightforward than planning a routine when you work irregular shifts, but life goes on, and you must manage it. Family, exhaustion, and friends all play a part in your lives and must be managed. Speak to them about what you want to achieve, and then be open and a bit selfish. Explain that you need to take some time for yourself. Be realistic, and be prepared to negotiate or offer a balanced solution. Use the Caveman Tribal Sorter to manage others more effectively. Plans become more manageable when people around you understand and support you. The fewer times that a plan gets challenged by others, the fewer chances that any wiggle room is created.

Being a cop, shift work was hard, but when I wanted to feel fitter, I found making changes more manageable when I had a diary.

Shift work is weird as it messes with your clock, so tacking on a gym session after a set of nights, dusting off the bike to cycle to work or taking in healthy food for breaks did not feel like a massive chore. It was part of the plan. It needed organisation, but keeping to the plan was more straightforward, and I managed to make it happen. What helped was sharing my digital calendar with my family so that they could see what I was doing and not have to ask or expect anything different.

Once you have a rigid plan, you can add the fun bits and plan the milestone rewards; writing them is covered in a later chapter. The Mammoth will not get excited watching a load of weights going up and down for an hour but will be motivated by the promise of a relaxing swim, a jacuzzi of something nice to look forward to. You have to be creative when motivating the Mammoth; reaching a weight goal will keep the Herder happy, but for the Mammoth, the promise of buying new clothes (do not restrict yourself to buying smaller sizes) is a sure way to keep it engaged. Offering a tasty smoothie or treat for every tenth visit makes the Mammoth want to play a winnable game.

Progress can and should only be stealthily recorded, especially when quitting smoking or other bad habits. Don't use a running chart; use a simple way to tally results later. For me, for every email I got confirming my CV was submitted, I moved it to its folder, not looking or counting until I hit a milestone. You should only look at the results when you break for a milestone and take the promised reward. Planning these triumphs into the route helps the Mammoth's motivation to keep going. However, if you keep checking the amount of work you have done each day and do not see any progress with a running total, you are showing no progress to your Mammoth, and your Herder will want to make a change. Herders want to find quick solutions to problems, and seeing this makes them despondent. They will find a shortcut to speed up results and want to derail the plan. The Mammoth is happy to keep going and wants a clear plan; they want to move toward the reward.

Letting the Mammoth focus on the reward is key. It has something to look forward to, and it is becoming a new and exciting habit in which it is keen to participate.

Keep the momentum going and stick to the promise; keep it focused on something nice it will enjoy, and even picture the reward to motivate yourself in stressful situations.

If you keep hitting the Mammoth's positive emotions, you keep the Herder's desire to change the plan at bay; you want them to lead the Mammoth. Motivation is not the Herders' problem; their problem is their focus, patience and commitment. The job of keeping your Mammoth calm is enormous. Sticking to the plan and keeping things moving forward is a massive responsibility. The job of the Herder is to ensure that the Mammoth feels comfortable and relaxed.

The objective for a change should be something more than hitting goals, as this is what only the Herder enjoys. Reaching a goal is a tiny part of the journey; it must be fun and fulfilling for the Mammoth's sake. This is the fundamental shift in the mind that we must be aware of if we want change to happen.

An interesting research project in 1971 that might impact your mindset of change was called the Stanford Prison Experiment. As a quick overview, it saw students being monitored in a fake prison in the University's basement. Half were told they were inmates, and the rest were nominated as prison guards. The outcome is still being debated today, but it showed that people act and react to the situation they find themselves in. Behaviours reflected the roles people played as an acceptable outcome of that situation. Guards were beating inmates, and even though they were friends only a few days before, the experiment had to be cancelled on the grounds of safety. It demonstrated that people do what people expect to do in certain situations. Mammoths are the worst for reacting to a bad situation; fat people do not belong in the gym, children from working-class families do not belong in universities, and the list goes on. This is nature versus nurture all over again.

If you believe that you are always going to be fat, a smoker or scared of ladders, this is the Mammoth talking. If you allow the Mammoth to continue to believe this, they will not change. Instead, it would be best to remove the Mammoth from this prison. Setting them free by getting them to focus on rewards rather than the process will take time and adjustment, but it is worth the effort.

No one likes doing anything alone. Mammoths are herd animals who follow their kind. If they have always been a cop and never thought they could do anything outside of their job, then they see a group of other cop Mammoths following their maps, each going down a path roughly heading in the same direction, it will want to join them. Utilising this by finding and using support groups is a huge boost. I joined the blue light leavers Facebook group. Never be afraid to do something because it might seem embarrassing; sign up for that dating site, join the timetabled group exercises at the gym, and make a pact to become part of the group, not just an attendee, hoping something will work.

Chat to the group; they are all there for the same reason. Be friendly, introduce yourself and motivate each other by agreeing to see them at the next meeting. It will motivate all involved to keep going, especially you. Giving the Mammoth a reason to be with its kind helps. If you show that it is not the only Mammoth to face these challenges and that other Mammoths are capable of the same journey, it will be more comfortable getting to the next milestone. Make sure your Herder does not pick the group.

THE CAVEMAN PRINCIPLES

They will push too hard, wanting to befriend Usain Bolt and asking to run with him, scaring the Mammoth. Pick the new herd carefully, research, test, and test again to see what works. Ignore your Herder's shouts to push harder and monitor your Mammoth. If the group is not correct, too easy, too hard, or just not for you, your Mammoth will not be motivated and will return to its old comfortable rut before you can do anything about it.

15.
PICTURE IT

Focus on the Mammoth.

The Herder can jump on and off different paths, try new things, and believe they are keeping their focus on the end goal, but if left to their own devices, they will never progress. Every time they change direction, the Mammoth loses interest and gets scared. The change of direction is too quick for any real change to happen. You may not want this to happen, but there is a high chance it will. When it does happen, you must be able to attract the Mammoth and bring it back to focusing on the goal. Mammoths only like doing something long-term; when they get lost, they lose their emotional attachment, making it hard for them to return to the path. Herders are gullible, a sucker for a quick win that only leads the Mammoth back to old habits. The Herder's job is to stay on the path, help lead the Mammoth, and take its mind off wanting to quit. Herders love new, shiny, tempting things and need a way to keep their attention on the agreed plan. You want the Herder to make the Mammoth comfortable with the change; then, over time, you want the change to become a Mammoth habit that can only be done when they work together.

The clearly defined route makes the Mammoth more comfortable. Using an emotional link to the outcome creates a positive change. The Mammoth needs the emotional motivation to start down the path and then a technique to not get put off when the Herder's curiosity makes it look down a new route. Using a picture is a reminder to keep it going, and it will cross the finish line before it knows it.

You will need to use a solid mental picture. Some call this manifesting, but it really sets our focus. The image must be easy to recall and used repeatedly to remind the Mammoth why the change is needed and why it must keep going. The image needs to have such a strong pull that any thought by the Mammoth of giving up is quickly ignored.

Rushing this stage is not an option. The picture must be perfect, not a 'that will do'. If you do this properly at the beginning, you run little risk of losing the Mammoth.

Your Herder also benefits from this exercise; you give it a tool to motivate the mammoth when it feels tired (willpower is low) and a reminder that the Herder must stay on track (no distractions). You must be able to see the picture and draw such a detailed mental picture that it makes it feel like a reality. You will want to use every trick, colour, and sense imaginable, including every feeling you could have. Then, you will link it as a trigger to recapture the Mammoth's attention and get it back on track.

You know what you want to achieve, and you already have it marked out in your plan, whether it is being slimmer and fitter, having more money, being happier and healthier, or holding a snake. As a result, you build a picture in your mind of how you will look when you complete this change.

As a snapshot, I saw myself as a successful project manager. I wore comfortable chinos, a smart shirt, and a quality jacket. I was smiling, feeling the responsibility of my work and a feeling that my effort was being put somewhere worthy. Every one of my emotions was attached to this outcome. The sense of doing something important made me feel proud, and of course, it reflected in my income, which was then part of the next part of my plan, rebuilding my home life. Linked was my reason to stop abusing alcohol, feeling good about myself and no longer needing to drown my sorrows. My picture was built far beyond these words, and I could see myself clearly, feeling all the emotions I could think of.

Adding as much background detail, you will see yourself as having that beach body, ripped muscles, a big white smile, or that look when you see a healthy bank balance. Where you will be and what you are doing becomes essential to the picture. Only you can make this image vivid, vibrant and lifelike. Tricks to help that image come together are precious memories, feelings, desires, wants and expectations. You will build it, flesh it out, and make it seem like your reality as if you are looking in a mirror. Before making it a solid thought, you must find a Caveman marker.

Using a physical item helps remind you of your picture. It should be something you can carry everywhere, an item just for this purpose (keys and wallets are not good). I used my old dog tag, a sentimental item I'd never lose.

Use a smooth stone, a button, something nice to hold, or anything that will stay in your pocket or with you when you are awake—this item will be your trigger switch.

Holding the Caveman marker in your hand, you will link it with your imagined picture. Then, every time you squeeze it, the sensation of the item will remind you of your picture. You will need to have your eyes closed and some uninterrupted time, so you will need to be somewhere quiet where you will not be disturbed. Don't do it just yet; finish reading the instructions.

When ready, with your eyes closed, hold the item, squeeze it or pinch it, feel not just the item but the way it pushes into the skin, and even if it makes your hand slightly hurt or ache, note the feeling. Savour it and get used to that unique feeling. Once you have your switch, squeeze the marker, start forming the picture of yourself; see your face and hair, and know it is you.

As an example, you need to see the fine detail. If you have hair, see it on your head, even your grey bits. Make it undoubtedly you. Now imagine the most enormous and happiest smile on your face, not a grin or a camera smile, but a big, fat smile of success and happiness. Feel the smile spread across your face, and embrace how that makes you feel. Give it a moment and then look at your eyes; they are happy, shiny and relaxed. Feel it for a moment and then move on to your body. Your body with your hands, arms, legs and toes. Feel the Caveman marker in your hand. Squeeze it.

Notice that your body already feels different. A little taller, you are walking tall, proud of your accomplishment, with your shoulders back and relaxed. Your thoughts acknowledge that you look different. Spend time doing this. Notice that you look better than ever, and let it sink in for a moment. Feel the Caveman marker in your hand.

Focus on the picture of you. This is when you are at your very best after accomplishing your goal. Add as much detail as possible, backgrounds and sunshine. Make it the happiest place you can imagine. Squeeze your marker. Make yourself visible in that now "known" happy place.

The surrounding images are bright; the picture makes you feel warm, safe, secure, and happy. Feel the weight of the Caveman marker in your hand.

Only when you get to this stage do you add depth to the picture, focusing on the result of the change. Add the feelings, the sense of accomplishment you have, being on top of the world, excitement, pride, like a god or semi-deity. Feel the power, focus, and hard work paying off to get you here. Add your change picture, and squeeze your marker. Imagine the fat belly gone, the urge for sugar, alcohol or smoke gone, and the feeling of walking past a fruit machine without the need to put a few coins in it. Hold the thought. How does it feel? How much do you want this feeling? Keep it there for as long as possible; get comfortable with the thought of change. Feel the weight of the Caveman marker in your hand. Squeeze it.

Focus back on the look on your face; see it smiling, then feel calm and invincible. You are happier than ever, with no care in the world. Stood, sat or relaxed in your happiest place. Without losing focus, bring yourself back to the now, feel all your senses, smell the air, gently touch your fingertips, feel the weight of your back push into the chair as you relax, check into your body, and feel how it reacted to this change in thought. Squeeze the marker and let your image flash up. Transfer your immediate feelings to the picture and back to life. Add all the feelings and make them strong. Your body might be holding itself up straighter and feeling determined. Acknowledge it and squeeze your marker.

Please focus on the required change. Imagine how your body feels when it has completed the challenge. Add extra levels to the results. Imagine finishing your race, maybe with a personal best time, the flat stomach that no longer stops you from seeing your feet, or even how the hard abs under your shirt feel against the material. Notice how your clothes fit, the giant arms showing through the shirt. Feel the extra weight of the money in your pocket. Take a large breath, feel your clean lungs expand, and absorb all the oxygen you need. Get, hold and sense the feeling of absolute achievement. Feel proud, feel good, and feel the Caveman marker in your hand. You are feeling happier than you have been for a long time.

When you have the fullest picture, sit with it, watch it, and check that all your senses are engaged and you feel joy.

When you feel fulfilled, focused, and clear, take a '3D snapshot' of the changed you.

Not just an image but adding the feelings, how you are feeling, the colours, and the senses. Squeeze your Caveman marker in your hand. Feel everything as you squeeze.

When you are done, open your eyes and look at your Caveman marker. Test it by squeezing it, and ensure you get your clear picture and feelings flash back into your head.

From now on, when you need a boost, close your eyes and squeeze your marker. See the same image and feel all those senses again. Linking your marker to your picture engages the Herder and the Mammoth. Keep your Caveman marker close to hand and in a safe place.

The Caveman marker is there to help you focus the Mammoth and its emotions. It is precious to you, so guard it and look after it. Should it be lost, forgotten, or misplaced, then not all is lost. Find a replacement item and go back over your linking exercise.

Try to find something of similar size, feel it, and keep squeezing it, but don't lose this one this time.

Now that you have a tool you can use to keep the Mammoth on track, you need to train the Herder. The Caveman marker is tuned to the Mammoth, but now we must trust the Herder to keep our snapshot image unchanged, safely rolled up, ready to use, and to hand. When the Mammoth loses interest in the new path, wanting to eat a doughnut, light a cigarette, or drop some money in a fruit machine, you will squeeze the marker. This is the signal for the Herder to use the image. Your unchanged and original focused snapshot is in the Herder's charge. The Herder may want to add new bits of information, but just like your original plan, don't let them change a thing. Use an imaginary glass frame to protect that image. You must watch and chastise the Herder if you see him doodling something extra onto the original, hence the glass covering to prevent this. Training the Herder to unroll the image, holding it up in front of the Mammoth's face, and making the Mammoth look at it is the reason for a hard squeeze. They are to hold it until all those emotions you linked to that image come through.

The Herder's job is to get the Mammoth to remember those feelings and the sense of achievement by showing the image. You want the Herder to use the image to motivate and calm the Mammoth. You need the Mammoth to start salivating and drooling over the end goal again, motivating it to want to keep moving forward.

Your snapshot image, linked to squeezing the Caveman marker, will keep hitting the Mammoth in its emotional gut and the Herder on the agreed path. The Mammoth will realise how much it wants the change and keep going. Not worrying about walking up a flight of stairs and having to stop to catch its breath to make things happen or about what it will spend all that extra cash on instead of giving it to the multi-million-pound gambling business, the squeeze is what is used to grab its attention back on the path. The image will help the Mammoth remember its goal and the promise to reach that destination and continue on the path with renewed enthusiasm.

Whatever picture you have created, make it strong and full of positive emotions. Avoid using negative thoughts or veiled threats if it is not achieved. Positive thoughts and kindness beat a beating. Do not cheat by lying to yourself. Painting a mental picture of a salad bowl and then convincing yourself that it tastes like a juicy steak will not work for long, but agreeing to find tasty dried fried onion crumbs to enhance the taste of a green leaf will. Honesty and being realistic are vital. Some people will never be as fast as Usain Bolt, but they can improve their running times. You should only measure your progress against yourself and never against someone else on a different journey. Everything you do has to motivate your Mammoth; it is not stupid, so treat it with respect and ensure you are happy and having fun; if you need more to keep things fun, you must complete the milestone chapter.

Mental images and the use of the Caveman marker are your best tools. You can boost your success by drawing or finding images that help your mind return to your internal picture. Images that inspire your change can be printed and placed in strategically located 'danger' places. A small picture of a piggy bank or dream holiday printed as a credit card-sized image popped in front of your bank card in your wallet can work wonders. A photo of a pair of your trainers or a designer shirt you want can be taped to the fridge door.

Motivational images and drawings of your dream are tucked into the front of your paperwork for work, or stuck on the lid of your laptop, or below your monitor. Use the linking exercise to make these images work like your marker; make them mean something more than a pretty piece of paper.

'Chuff' charts, where you track progress, are not good. They will only remind you of the daily slog. The daily struggles will nag at your Mammoth, making it think it will never reach its desired weight loss, and it will give up. You should be looking forward to and using milestone checks instead. Using a photo of your last holiday when you were on the beach, with your stomach bulging over your shorts, that you have taped to the fridge door, or that classy picture of you having a cigarette hanging out of your mouth and placed near the back door might seem like a good idea but don't do it. You need to keep it positive. You want to present the change that you want or need. Make the Mammoth want to keep the promise, not be the constant negative nag that will drag it to failure.

If you struggle when taking your snapshot picture, using the following 'miracle' question is a great way to help create that mental and physical picture.

> *"Imagine that in the middle of the night, while you were sleeping, a miracle happened, and all the troubles you want to change were resolved. When you wake up, how will you know something has changed, and how will you feel about it?"*

Understanding what works for you is necessary, and some trial and error will be involved. You must be open to learning a few new skills, as everything you have done up to this point has not yet achieved your desired result. Getting depth and perception is key, so a short story to make a point.

A blind man sat on the busy footpath. He had an empty bucket and a sign hanging above his head. He was collecting money for charity. A white stick was displayed, and a handwritten sign said, "Blind, please help." No one stopped, and everyone ignored the sign.

Another man sat across the street, drinking a coffee and watching the blind man and everyone walk past him. This man found another piece of cardboard and wrote a new message. Crossing the road, not saying a word to the blind man, he propped the new sign over the original. He dropped some money in the bucket and walked away.

When the man left, people started to put money in the bucket, which continued until it overflowed. Then, people began to put money in the blind man's hand.

The blind man was so emotionally overcome that he asked one person why they were doing this. The person said that it was because of the sign, and they wanted to help. The blind man said, "What, my sign that reads 'Blind, please help'?" The donor said, "No, it reads, 'It's a beautiful day. You can see it, I cannot." Emotion rules over request; it works better than demand. You must change your thoughts from problem-focused, "My trousers are too tight," to solution-focused, "My trousers will fit much better when I lose weight."

The new path becomes more comfortable when the Mammoth emotionally understands what, why, and how change is needed. Images, reminders, and triggers all help it stay on track. The Mammoth likes being safe and enjoys a habit. When you show that the new habit has a positive effect, the Mammoth suddenly becomes committed. The image is about making the Mammoth want it, that any failure means not reaching the destination, and it loses those desired emotions and feelings.

The Caveman marker, images and pictures should be used when a change starts, progresses, stumbles, reaches milestones, and when needed to maintain your focus. Keeping the Mammoth on the new path takes effort and many squeezes; practice becomes a habit. Things get easier as you progress. The constant use of the marker will start to wane, meaning the Herder will be holding up the image less often. Evaluating and recognising the lack of squeezes is a simple fix if you feel unmotivated or want to give up; this could be the reason. Refocus and do the linking exercise to refresh the image and keep going.

Emotional images are one of the strongest motivational pulls. When you reach the milestone chapter, you will use these images to keep the Mammoth on the path. Grab your camera, overcome your insecurities, and prepare an album to show the Mammoth how far it has come.

THE CAVEMAN PRINCIPLES

16.
MANAGING RESISTANCE

Time to tweak the plan.

Resistance to change is a challenge most will face. Unwillingness or a lack of wanting to change is difficult to understand. However, this will highlight why it needs addressing.

A scorpion wanted to cross a stream and saw a frog sitting on the bank. The scorpion asked the frog if it could ride across the stream on its back, but the frog declined, saying that if the scorpion were on its back, it would sting the frog.

The scorpion reasoned that if that were true, then both would perish. The frog thought about it and agreed that the scorpion had a point. It allowed the scorpion to ride on its back and started swimming across the stream.

Halfway across, at the deepest point, the scorpion stung the frog. The frog, succumbing to the poison, managed its last few words, asking, "Why did you break your promise?" The scorpion knew its fate and replied, "Because it is my nature."

The story resonates with people who believe they cannot change and want to use an excuse to refuse to change their ways, resisting because they have always done it this way. People like to sabotage their dreams and sometimes those of others because of stubborn personal beliefs.

The scorpion claimed it could change its nature and even convinced another that it could. The failed experiment was unfortunate for both, but a great reminder that some things may need more work.

Resistance is simply the Mammoth not wanting to move because others do it or because it has listened to someone giving an opinion. It has gotten stuck, worried, scared, and confused. Your job is to clear these obstacles, calm any concerns, and clear the way so your Mammoth can see the path again.

Lack of support or shrouded care from others, known as 'blag', is one of our Mammoth's biggest potholes.

This is one reason why telling friends in a social group that we want to lose weight or to get fit never happens.

Imagine telling someone in a pub you want to improve your health by reducing your drinking and bringing about a positive change. You probably know that most of your friends will laugh in your face. It makes you feel ridiculous for even thinking about it, and then if you did, you know they will ridicule you for weeks for mentioning that the change was a good idea.

If you believe you know how most of your friends will react, you will never use these valuable change networks. What if you can get them to support you and even join in? Would that help? Having a large part of your tribe stand behind you and wanting to remain friends is a huge benefit. This can be scary, as you must be honest with them and explain the consequences of not achieving the goal. If you can do this, it can boost your chances of success. Buy them all a copy of this book and link Part 2, using their personality traits to your advantage.

A Hunter friend will always want to compete. Use this to add a competitive edge to the conversation and make them want to join the challenge.

If it is a Protector, use them to help organise the change. Ask them for their opinion, what they know, and how they would achieve it. Make them the planners and get them to manage the tribe's social diary. Give them responsibility and make sure they know the desired outcome. You'll need this to get them to want to walk the new path with you.

Gatherers are the more unsocial ones, and it will take a lot of work to get them to buy into any joint group effort. But if you want them to be part of it, ask them to do the research and tell them you'll all want to do it their way. There may be compromises, but they can become great motivators. Make them the authoritative knowledge figures, and ask them to research the best training, route, or food.

Healers love it when they get emotionally involved. The best way to get them to join the quest is to open up to them. Telling a Healer a personal secret of why you need to make the change allows them to care; they will suddenly want to help. Making it more personal by adding your feelings about why you want to lose weight, stop smoking, or any other reason, and explaining your thoughts if you can't make this change happen, will get them involved. Asking for their help after doing this will be enough. They will feel obliged to watch over you and even mentor you.

You can also use them as a complementary therapist, confiding in them when you are struggling, slipping or falling off the wagon. They will be the ones who pick you back up, motivating you to try again and keep going.

If you think those last few paragraphs are too far-fetched, the fact that you call these people your friends should be enough to trust them. However, if they do not support you, then you must consider an extreme option and cut them out of your life.

Just reading this part of the book, it is evident that you need to make a change, and if your friends are a barrier to that change, you must make a choice. Changing your life sometimes requires sacrifice and dedication; if your friends don't want you to change, then you must change your friends.

If they are unwilling to support a positive change, especially if it will make you a better person, they will probably be a factor in why you constantly fail. Bad friends come ten to the penny; they use any opportunity to drag you down. Most of the time, they fear any change and will fight anyone who mentions the word. Considering whether they are true friends is up to you. A real friend is someone you can rely on for their support, someone who goes out of their way and comes to London to attend your book launch or moves into your home for a week to make sure you are OK, regardless of the impact it makes in their life.

If they don't, perhaps you need to make a friend change before making a personal change. After publishing this book in 2015, several people I considered friends moved on, and I have never missed them; in reflection, things are better now that they are no longer in my life.

You must dig deep when you encounter resistance and check everything you do, as it will impact you. There is no need to have another go at our plan because someone is unwilling to move.

No matter how many plans you create, something else will hold you back. If you are not progressing, there will be a reason. If you are honest with yourselves, you will know what that is. You always do it to yourself, but you ignore it or make excuses for it and see it as an unmovable object because you do not want to tackle it. If you're going to make an actual change, you must swallow that frog. No matter how uncomfortable conversations become, you have only yourself to answer to. Most of the time, these concerns or problems are resolved quickly and do not cause vast amounts of pain. It can be a misunderstanding or fear of embarrassment rather than resistance, but you will only know this when you deal with it.

If this has reached a level deeper than the scope of this book, you may need to seek help from a trained professional.

One last area to check for resistance is your environment. A great example is if you want to stop smoking, it will be easier if you stop hanging around the smoking areas. If you always buy a cake or chocolate bar from the same shop or petrol station, consider using a different shop or start cycling.

If you always buy fast food from a drive-through you pass on your way home, changing the route will help take these enticements away. Think about all the habits the Mammoth enjoys and what you can do to make it easier not to remember and avoid them. Mammoths want us to keep doing the same thing, so challenge any negative thoughts about why you must stick to the route. It likes to stay in its comfort zone and wants us to make life easy. Making excuses as to why this cannot happen is one of its tricks. Don't succumb to its whines and complaining. Use the Caveman marker, let the Herder do its job and show the mental image; get the Mammoth comfortable with why the change is needed.

Without tackling these resistance problems, you will be subjected to the Mammoth's constant blockers; it will be energy-sapping, and you will eventually give in. Never underestimate how much power and strength a massive Mammoth has. Without managing the concerns, blockages, and troubles, letting it have so much control over your thoughts can derail any progress. Deal with it positively, and do not give in because it is easier.

You are not alone, as resistance is a genuine concern for all readers of The Caveman Principles.

If you fail, it will be because the Mammoth has given up. You must check everything and ensure it is not the people around you. If it's not them, check if it is the environment. If it's not your surroundings, check for any poor nurturing or unwitting subconscious training you have been exposed to. Some resistance issues will need to be explored further, but the fundamental principles are the same: discover why your Mammoth does not want you to move forward.

17.
CELEBRATE THE MILESTONES

Make the journey enjoyable.

You should be set for your new path, and now you all need to make it fun and get the Mammoth to focus ahead. The journey will be long and sometimes unappetising, especially if you try to make it to the end in one go. Using a gaming analogy, you must set save points for rest and refuelling. These will be part of your route and are called milestone targets. This is where you can pick things up again if you go off the path. Setting these smaller targets saves you from chasing the Mammoth back to the beginning and allows you to jump from one to the next in more bite-sized chunks. They will lead you one step at a time to the end game and your eventual victory.

Convincing the Mammoth to start down a new path has taken a lot of effort and preparation. You cannot expect it to do something so huge and to try something it has never achieved before; you must make it seem possible to achieve. Your Herder and the Mammoth are a team; they have shaped the path together. Your image is in your head; the Herder knows when to show it. Squeezing the caveman marker is all great, but how do you keep the Mammoth focused and motivated for an extended period? You make it fun.

Mammoths do not like being out of their depth. You must ensure that the journey is exciting and enjoyable and that there are quick, sustainable wins to keep things moving. Mammoths get bored, and changing a Mammoth's habit after years of the same routine is difficult.

If you have never been to a gym and set yourself a target of being able to do 100 press-ups, you cannot expect to do them all straight away. You need to build up to the 100. Being able to do ten by the end of the first week, fifteen the week after and ultimately, months later, if you can do the 100 press-ups in one exercise, then you have worked out that you have to pencil in your milestones. An increment of 5 can be a milestone achieved, a small win, where you can see progress. If you can see this working, using this theory can make every other change you want more manageable.

When you set the Mammoth off down the new path, you want to offer it treats as emotional rewards at intervals where you think it needs a morale boost. These are prearranged stops, milestones along the path, set at stages where you want to start seeing some results.

Imagine driving a car from one end of the UK to the other, all 847 miles. Until now, no car or driver could travel that distance without stopping and refuelling. Would many drivers want the challenge of driving that distance without stopping?

You can imagine the Mammoth and the Herder being motivated to do the press-ups or the 847 miles. They are pumped, excited and determined. They start in earnest, smiling, breathing the air and feeling invincible. When things get tough, they start feeling tired, so they use the image, squeeze the caveman marker, and get a slight boost. They manage to keep themselves going, but ultimately, disaster happens. The Mammoth gets tired and bored, and there is nothing that you can do to keep it motivated; it just gives up.

It did not have the option to rest and continue afterwards. Instead, it returned to its comfortable rut and refused to get back on the path because it was not fun and too challenging.

Mammoths like winning, not failure. Milestones give the Mammoth a break with something it can focus on that is not out of its grasp. Quick milestone wins keep it in the game, enticing it to go that little bit further each time it gets a win and keep it in the mindset of the long haul.

Earlier, you read about not letting the Mammoth look behind and being reminded of the lack of progress it makes from a day-to-day perspective. If allowed, the Mammoth will watch the progress and not recognise the slow change taking effect. Instead of motivating, it sees little or no daily progress and will not enjoy the feeling of failure. Instead, you must focus on the next milestone, looking ahead. No one stays on the path or makes significant progress when all they do is look in the rear-view mirror, so only check it when it is safe.

Milestones must be planned along the route to mark noticeable, small achievements. The route and destination might be having big, strong arms like Arnie Schwarzenegger, but as an average Joe, this is not a quick win without cheating and using steroids. The Mammoth needs to focus on the next set of weights or the next shirt size. How about the subsequent measurement of the biceps? Whatever you wish to plan as the next step should not be the final milestone until your plan dictates it.

Milestones work both ways. You must watch the Herder, as sometimes they do not think about the route and can ruin progress with one foolish act of wanting to speed things up. They will jump ahead of their available ability and destroy self-confidence by overextending or fixing a win, such as taking laxatives to lose weight. Or they will stupidly put 250 kg on a bar and want the Mammoth to do it immediately. As the Mammoth trusts the Herder, it will try and probably fail. The trust will be instantly broken, and the Mammoth suddenly feels like a fool, letting the side down; it gets scared and embarrassed. The Herder, wanting to push things over the milestone line, has shown the Mammoth that the task is impossible. Loss of faith and feeling of pointlessness comes over the Mammoth, and it goes straight back to its comfortable rut, no longer wanting to try.

Herders will want to leapfrog forward and complete milestones quicker, believing they can get you to finish earlier than planned. Their purpose is to try, but they can fixate on achieving a milestone and not making it fun, rather than the long haul and the desired outcome. They do not think about the pressure this puts on the Mammoth or how it ruins the agreed path and journey.

Do not let the Herder jump along the path too quickly. Ensure they understand it has to be fun and get them to accept each step and commit to one step at a time. The Herder should focus on giving care and purpose to the Mammoth and making it fun. When they get ahead of themselves, make them look at the journey, read the map, and see the next milestone and how they will get to it.

As you progress and when you hit your first milestone, it will give instant gratification to the Mammoth, motivating it to keep going. Herders can derail this progress, so don't let them. There is no harm in gently pushing the Mammoth, but putting things like finite dates on achievements is not wise, as things can be pushed too hard.

This can be difficult as some things, such as weddings and specific engagements, are time-sensitive. Ultimately, you need to focus on making progress. Any progress is better than none. Using the tools and moving forward should be the only goals.

Stating what you want to achieve by the end of this week might be dangerous. If you are unsuccessful because life gets in the way, things happen, or we put the line too high, you will fail to make any change. All this has come from the Herder's perspective of pushing too hard. You must be able to monitor your short-term change, refocus and keep trying. Failing to reach a milestone by a specific date is the end for the Mammoth, marking the whole change as 'Game Over', so don't do it.

When the Mammoth reaches each milestone, make a big deal about it. Getting your Herder to celebrate it with the Mammoth is a way of focusing the team. Doing something that you enjoy makes a great motivating impact on the journey. If you have given up smoking for a month, celebrate it by doing something of value and fun, be inventive, and make it an authentic experience.

Use the money from not buying cigarettes and go out for the day, or go for a meal with friends and family, something you will remember. Experience and memories will outperform buying things and trinkets; things will be forgotten, and trinkets lost, but memories stick and will keep the mind focused on the end goal. Whatever you do, make sure you have good memories and the milestone is celebrated in a fun way.

If you like to share and leverage social media support (unless this is the change you want to achieve, you may want to skip this paragraph), post about your completed milestone. What you did, upload photos and tag people as a reminder of the great work you have achieved. These will generate comments, likes, and shares. If used properly, they will boost your Mammoth's emotional motivation, keeping things fresh in your mind. Making the journey a live document where others can participate creates pride in your achievements. All this can work wonders for motivation.

What you want to achieve is for the Mammoth to stop, take stock of the progress, celebrate, recharge, and get ready for the next milestone.

Keeping a record of your progress, ticking chuff charts and constantly checking to see how far you have come is not motivational. Weighing yourself daily and marking your weight loss chart will not be sustainable, as it will not show significant progress. At the start, it will probably be great, but when it plateaus out, crossing off each pound lost becomes unmotivating when nothing happens for days. Plan to weigh yourself weekly or even fortnightly. If the chart marks when you stopped smoking, counting the number of smoke-free days is just a cruel reminder of what you have deprived yourself of. Counting in months is easier, or how your taste buds have returned to life is a celebration. When you want to change your job, putting your CV out there and counting the number of recruiters, job interviews, rejections, and phone calls reminds you that job hunting is hard and turns off the Mammoth. Instead of micromanaging the change, focus on each milestone. From the first achievement to the very last one, get the Mammoth to mentally picture the journey and keep it motivated to get to the next one and then the next.

A simple motivation technique is to make the Mammoth feel the joy and excitement of achieving every milestone through celebration; it will want to get to the next one. Before you know it, the Mammoth is being led by the Herder and crossing the finishing line. The path has taken them through change and into their new life. When a journey has been broken into smaller, more manageable chunks, the distance will feel like a short haul.

My milestones were to get my CV out there, let the plan run, post it where agencies and recruiters would find it, refresh it weekly, and then take stock of whether I received phone calls and offers of interviews. Interviews turned into job offers, and offers were rejected or accepted. But I made sure each one was celebrated, representing a step in the right direction: cinema tickets, dinner out, a new jacket, going on holiday.

With money now coming in, my milestones extended to buying a house, and then I spent three years renovating it, so there were loads of milestones for each task, room, and completion stage when accomplished. Takeaways, new furniture, a once-in-a-lifetime trip, weekends in London. Each milestone was marked and remembered.

I knew doing up a house was a long slog, and only when I had completed it could I concentrate on my business, so I could give it my all: grow the speaking business, celebrate being picked up by speaking agencies, and have this book republished. Each step came with memorable celebrations.

I have many more milestones to go, but you can see how you can make your challenge more fun and motivating. Planning milestones is an essential part of the journey. Putting milestones into the change acts as easy markers for the Mammoth to focus on. You want to motivate and encourage it to continue along the journey and to be self-motivated to reach the next one, so do something fun.

Changing a milestone should not be done, but it needs a delicate touch if there is an absolute need. I advise you never to change one, but if you do, you must handle this grenade carefully. When you have tried everything to keep things going, and it is hard to keep focused, it is because of inexperience and poor planning. Do not despair.

When the Mammoth flags, slows and feels spooked, it is time to take action.

You do not want to overuse the Caveman marker; as a tool, you want it to be effective throughout the journey and not worn out. It is time to reassess a milestone. If it is a real struggle to get to the next one, you do not want to let the Mammoth give up and quit, so you must act.

Re-evaluating the next milestone might be wise; breaking it into two might be the answer to regain momentum if it is too far away. The warning of doing this is that it cannot be done too often.

When a mid-milestone is reached, celebrations need to match the reduced progress, but the full milestone still needs to be celebrated in full.

Celebrating all milestones is uplifting for the Mammoth. We do not want it to think it can slack off and still get the same reward. That extra weight may be too much on this occasion, so celebrate the halfway point and keep things moving. It is key to ensure you do not hand a win to the Mammoth; it must work for it.

Finding a one-off, different milestone is an option, a distinct occasion for it to celebrate. Do not add these as a regular occurrence, as it will detract and start to take the Mammoth off the path and into the danger zone. Count how many gym sessions have been completed since the start of the journey. Find something that the Mammoth can be proud of. Let it show off the progress it has made, how many sets of stairs you can climb without getting out of breath, how much easier it is to put on a pair of old jeans, how much closer we can get toward our toes, anything that it can show as an improvement.

Call it a motivational milestone, as this will tell the Mammoth that it is not part of the plan and must work towards the original one.

The gaming save point is your last milestone achievement. It can be used as your safety net. Milestones are significant for motivation, and they are also helpful as a restart point. If something spooks the Mammoth, and it wants to run back toward the comfortable rut, you can coax it back to its last successful milestone. You need to stop the Herder pushing forward without the Mammoth. The Herder must accept a minor setback and stop the Mammoth from throwing in the towel. It is a chance to take a collective breather, think about things, assess progress and conclude that it has already come a long way. That giving up is not an option. Squeeze the Caveman marker and let the Herder use the image to get the Mammoth's attention again. They need to bring their focus back to their destination, and they need to keep going forward.

The Mammoth will need space and time to calm down and see reason. At the milestone, let it feel the progress, remember the fun memories, and feel proud of its achievements.

Pushing the Mammoth back on the path must be carefully managed, or it will get spooked again. It may need time to get comfortable, feel the benefit of the change, and become motivated to take the next step.

Moving toward the next milestone will require careful management. Take it easy, as the Mammoth will be more anxious until it achieves the next Milestone. Get the Herder to slow down, not push the Mammoth. Walk it steadily to the next milestone and take the pressure off yourself. When the Mammoth passes that milestone, celebrate it like no other. Make a huge deal about it, get the excitement building in the Mammoth as it gets closer, and show that the last milestone was worth the effort to keep going.

Milestones must be part of change; it is not a race, so don't let the Herder push ahead too fast. The end game is getting the Mammoth to cross the finishing line. Using milestones along the journey is a huge motivational opportunity. Let all the planned milestones combine to make the one significant change happen.

18.
REACH THE DESTINATION

Break the habit.

Change is a stressful process when it is not managed correctly, the Mammoth gets spooked, and we push our button. All Mammoths need to be managed differently. What works for one may not work for another. What is clear is that doing the same thing as others, hoping to get the same results, means you have not learnt anything about these giant furry beasts. Feel free to try again, following someone else's plan, but expect the same results. Change the process and the setting and personalise the route next time, and you'll see that the same big picture is not right for you.

Done right with all the work and dedication you need to put into the planning, setting up every element before starting down the right path will lead to the desired change. Too many people embark on a change journey and do not realise how much preparation work is needed; do not be one of them.

You know about the five P's:" Proper Planning Prevents Poor Performance;" these are just as important when you want an essential change in your life. If you line up at the start of a Marathon without preparing, you know what will happen; maybe for the first few miles, you'll be ok, but then the journey gets more demanding as you have not trained, planned and understood what was needed. You throw in the towel and are disappointed you did not complete the 26 miles. If you are serious about change, treat it like a marathon and do the work before you step off the start line.

The destination may be to lose weight, stop smoking, get fitter, be a better parent by helping your child with homework, treat the love of your life with more respect and compassion, or get a better job. Whatever it is, each change requires a different focus and preparation. Regardless of the change, you are the only person who controls the pace, direction, and success.

Whatever the change, make sure you set the right intent, map the path, give it meaning, and draw a picture for the Mammoth. Use all the senses.

The Herder must lead, coax, and calm the Mammoth, not resort to pushing it. Willpower will disappear long before the Mammoth makes any dent in the journey; it must make up its mind. Make sure each milestone is set in stone, counted, and recorded. Both Herder and Mammoth must remain together. Don't let the Herder run off when they see the finishing line; keep them both on track and together. The finishing line is just as crucial in the journey as all the little bits completed on the path; focus on the right part of the journey at the right time. Motivating the Mammoth will be hard; keeping it motivated is harder. But when some momentum starts, things get easier, but do not let your guard down. If you move away from the finishing line, milestones, or the intent of the change, the Mammoth will get spooked, lose interest, and run back to its comfortable rut.

The Caveman Change Principles need to be followed. Make that commitment. Habits are hard to break. Think of the addiction cycle, and do not be hard on yourself. Failing to make change happens. If you do not modify your route on your next attempt, the constant 'failures' will become a habit. Reset and check everything before you make the next plan.

The Caveman Change Principles will only work if you follow each stage, work out, plan, write down, religiously follow the plan and, most importantly, make it fun. Do not think there is no harm in improving the plan when it is in motion; if you do, it will fail. Stick to the agreed-upon plan. Finish the journey before you make any amendments.

Crossing the finishing line has to be the biggest celebration of the journey. Use the saved money or bend the credit card to ensure a proper celebration; whatever you do, make it memorable and fun. Doing this will show the Mammoth what success looks like and make them want to do it again. Never extend a route by adding to the plan. Finish the last one and create a new one. Start the process all over again; only this time, things might be easier because you know what you are doing.

Success breeds success. Mammoths love to win, and when they realise they have done something massive, such as making a real change, they will have an emotional link to the success and an ongoing interest in trying something else. Be ready to complete another change, and ensure you are prepared. When anyone has done something significant, like running their first marathon, parachuting from a plane, or losing four stone in weight, they immediately feel euphoric and want to do another challenge. Strike while the iron is hot, get the Mammoth when it is motivated and set about another change, improve what you have done or make another life change that you have always wanted to do.

Keeping the Mammoth calm is a skill. The more you do this, the easier it becomes. Recognising when such a situation arises is a great success. Create a plan for when Mammoths get spooked, and ensure you use milestones and markers. Stick to the plan and remove the fear of failure.

Use all the tricks you have read in this chapter: images, caveman markers, milestones—everything will help remind the Mammoth why it signed up and why it must keep going. Read the messages posted by people who supported you, look at your savings account, see that you no longer have yellow fingers and recognise how far you have come. Use all the positives as reminders of why your Mammoth cannot return to the starting line.

Keep the Mammoth on track and show how far it has come at the milestone save points. Please keep it going in the right direction. Keep the Herder under control. Remind them that they have signed a promise and must stay at the side of the Mammoth. Train the Herder when you use the Caveman marker; keep them in check. Ensure the Herder does not try to take a shortcut, change the route, run ahead, or do something stupid; remind them that they will lose the Mammoth and that all the effort, time, and motivation have so far been well-spent.

Issues will always pop up, but do not let them be excuses. There will always be resistance to manage, so manage it. People will do anything to derail the Herder and the Mammoth's chances because they fear change and want to keep things as they are. Don't let these resistant people change your destiny. Stay focused and stick to the plan.

Bringing all the chapters of this book to a final paragraph or two means that you now understand where stress comes from, that you are already less stressed and can manage the hidden Stress Mammoths. Your ability to communicate and manage people's expectations with the Caveman

Tribal Sorter has removed so much stress from your life that you suddenly have space to think for yourself. Finally, with the new positive changes you can make in your life, you can start to feel better, richer, and more appreciated than ever.

You've got this. Good luck, and never give up.

For useful downloads, newsletters, more learning opportunities or booking me for motivational speaker events or workshops, please visit:

www.elevatedtraining.org
or
www.carljones.org
And, of course,
www.cavemanprinciples.com

19.

BONUS BITS

How it came to be.

Chances are you want to rush off and try out a few things. This is a little bonus to help explain why you have this book in your hands, and my publisher, Chris Day at Filament publishing, requested that I add it. I wrote this book for a reason, and even with the Police trying to stop it from being published, it has succeeded in more ways than I have ever expected. If you're not interested in the personal story behind the words, skip these pages and start your new life. Good luck! But you will miss some juicy stuff, so if you're still reading, let's get into it.

All my life, I have wanted to help people, and I don't know why or how I ended up becoming a Cop, but stranger things have happened. I suppose wearing a hat gave me a purpose and an identity. Then, just like Pringles, I could not stop and started to collect more. I wanted to see how many I could wear.

I joined the Police in 2000, which gave me opportunities I never knew I wanted or knew were available. I got to wear many hats, the most memorable ones being riot control, counter-terrorism search, chemical-biological-radioactive-nuclear responder, fed rep, and detective.

Then, in 2009, the police ran out of hats I wanted to wear, so I used my free time to find a few more.

Joining 4624 Squadron in the Royal Air Force, I became a weekend warrior, a Reservist. Some may think getting a new hat was extreme, but I enjoyed wearing the RAF headgear more. They all had a purpose, from my beret to my Kevlar helmet, not forgetting my 'number 1' cap.

When I wore one of my hats, I was filled with pride. My chest felt slightly larger, and there was a real purpose. I thought that I was a part of something; I felt complete.

Both organisations gave me plenty of opportunities to experience life. From attending dangerous and thrilling police incidents, being called out for riot control, searching buildings for dignitary visits, and being sent to Afghanistan to load aeroplanes in the heat. Wow, what a life.

These hats distinguished me from being just another person in public. Juggling these hats, people thought I was crazy for doing all this. They'd say, "You are crazy!" So I'm sure I got their opinion right.

Laughing and enjoying my life, I carried on, doing two jobs. I found fulfilment. None of these hats caused me any stress, even when I wore them during times others could not even dream of.

No stress whilst in the middle of a 'bring your own bricks' riot or in the 'heat' of the Afghanistan desert during the summer months. My training covered these problems. These hats were my identity; I trusted them, and I cherished being part of something that I considered to be worthy.

My family and friends told me I was burning the candle at both ends. They tried to put doubt in my mind. They told me I had no downtime and could not be myself because my constant 'on the go' lifestyle could not be sustained.

2011 was when everything changed for me, responding to a domestic incident. During the arrest of a young lad called Ricky, because he had punched his girlfriend in the face. Then, from out of nowhere, he pulled a handgun and shot at me 6 times. I managed to detain him, restrain him and even secure the gun. No one was physically injured, but I didn't know what other forms of injury had been caused. He went to prison, and I was nominated to attend Number 10 for a national Bravery Award. Meeting with Theresa May and wandering around this magnificent building was terrific.

Not a year passed before I started to become ill. I was not sleeping, not feeling myself, and no longer enjoying anything; life became a real struggle. Getting up in the mornings and doing what I wanted was almost impossible. I kept wearing my hats, but a big chunk of me was missing; I felt incomplete. I always found a way to fix things and wanted to return to normal, so I started my investigation.

While I tried to find a solution, a change of management in the Police caused frustrations.

I was refused leave, which I needed for my RAF training, and the support ebbed away. After a few months of nonattendance, my Squadron Commander asked me to submit an early termination report. Handing in my kit, it felt like another piece of me was being ripped away. That was the end of my military life.

My Police work became my sole purpose once again, no other distraction. I had some free time, so I hit the books, did some soul searching, and even had some counselling sessions. It took a few years to get here, and I know I can save others from working all this out; the results are all in this book. The spoiler is that the source of my illness was not me; it was my reaction to life events—a combination of stress and, at the time, an underlying and undiagnosed PTSD illness.

The content of this book is from my research and, more importantly, from my experience as a cop. I had a front-row seat, watching how people responded to stress, criminal activity, and being caught. All the reactions you'd expect, plus an extra level of research, as when they were at their very worst, their reactions are more extreme.

Every day, suspects and victims showed me their true personalities as they desperately tried to understand things. These people were experiencing all manner of emotions and stress, and I was there doing my job, but also making notes on what I was witnessing.

My interest in people-watching finally paid off. I had always found it fascinating to watch how people interacted with each other. How quickly things can change when people become stressed, friendships easily broken, and even new alliances are made when needed. What these people did and, more interestingly, when I interviewed them, what they thought they were doing was fascinating. I discovered a new interest and outlet, and it was right there in my old job.

Most people are uncomfortable with being forthright and asking for what they want. Throw in some stress, especially in my work environment, and I could watch and start to predict what would happen. They all acted and reacted differently but also in a similar, predictable way. I realised there were some common responses and ended up researching human psychology. Myers-Briggs was my first read, along with William Marston, which led me to study the origins of categorising people. I found that Hippocrates (the most famous Greek Physician c.460-c.370 BC) had used 'four humours,' which still reflect today's modern theories. This personality profiling has been around for over 2,000 years, and I had just discovered it for myself.

With a new interest and a thirst for understanding, I put people in boxes, each showing unique character traits. My theories were being formed from my research and the individuals I interacted with daily. After some practice, I could identify a personality within a minute or two, improving my interactions and getting better results. My job got easier, and my stress levels started to reduce.

Speaking to victims, suspects, colleagues, and even my managers started to get easier. I began to like some people more and others a lot less. As I continued to test and understand how people worked and operated, I became more interested in the subject.

I used my new technique to communicate better, give meaning to what was happening around me, and gain new friends I once thought I'd never like. I could work people out faster, learn their true thoughts and feelings, and use them to my advantage. I could anticipate their wants and needs, which allowed me to become a better person and a better Police Officer. It was fun and even exciting to have an opportunity to work all this out.

Personality profiling was not my only research of choice. My understanding of stress and managing personal change needed to be significantly improved. These were complex subjects, making it difficult because no one wanted to explain how easy it could be. This stuff should be taught in schools; people need to be aware of the impact, but when things are too complicated, people become despondent and choose to ignore the subject. I wanted a new way to use all the information I had just learned and practised. How can it be made a fun, exciting and accessible subject? Then I found the how. All my research came together just as I found what I had been looking for.

Cavemen! My theories fit perfectly. I had my tribe, my new profiling tool, and tips on managing daily stress and making future goals more achievable; it worked a treat.

THE CAVEMAN PRINCIPLES

Putting it all together, I had The Caveman Principles. It was a brilliant icebreaker, and many people I shared my theories with became lifelong friends. Over Christmas in 2014, I met Becks on a holiday. Later, she contacted me via email. I remember when she was impressed with my theories and loved the detail of my characters. We had spent some time profiling other guests and hotel staff, with her going off to check. She asked me to write down my theories so she could use them in the future.

In her email, Becks told me she started using my theories when she returned from holiday. She returned to work, used the new profiling skills, and found a fantastic way to interact with her boss. She said she had gotten herself promoted within a month, something she had been unable to do for many years before we met. She said it was all because of my stress management and communication system that I had taught her in the bar.

This was when I truly believed I had something special. I had something I could teach people, even when the classroom was an alcohol-selling bar. This stuff was gold.

I started delivering talks to groups and began writing this book. It felt great to know I was helping people, as Beck's words still rang in my ears.

It was fun and easy. We can shape our future even when we live busy, stressful lives. My mantra is that the only person holding me back is me.

Developing the Caveman Principles improved my life, and I knew that once I shared them, they would also help others.

2024 - Update since this book was first published.
After jumping through all the correct hoops and getting the Police to authorise my business interest, it became the first edition, published in 2015. I happily went to book fairs and events for the next few years, sold quite a few copies, and loved chatting with people. I had some great speaking opportunities and had fun delivering my Caveman theories.

Unfortunately, my Mental Health took a dive, and in 2017, I was diagnosed with PTSD resulting from a combination of incidents, but the primary catalyst was the gun incident in 2011.

Every therapy I tried failed; I was stuck with this illness. A deep and unpleasant condition that no one, including the sufferer, understands. Over the next two years, the Police did not know what to do with me; instead of providing support, I was moved from department to department and disciplined for writing this book, which they had been happy to support.

I was still working as a cop, as this was all I knew, and it was paying the bills; I was suffering daily triggers and was burnt out. My days off were my outlet, a chance to speak to people about my theories, and as it had nothing to do with the work of the Police, it was my relief and only source of 'normal'.

Faced with internal disciplinaries related to this publication, believing the sole purpose was to stop this book from being sold, I knew it was my only life-saving outlet, and I did not want to give it up. After nineteen years of dedicated service and a "no case to answer" result from the numerous disciplines, I was medically retired from the police.

This should have been the end, but the aftermath was horrendous. It resulted in me losing everything in my professional and personal life.

Being forced to adjust to these changes, I faced a sink-or-swim moment—a chance to lie down and give up or use the time to reset the board and then have another go. Only this time, I had an advantage: my Caveman theories. I tested them once again, using them through these challenging times. Now I am back!

As I write this, it is 2024, I am remarried, have a beautiful, fully renovated home, and have a new career as an Innovation project manager. 2025 this edition will be republished, and it will be time to relaunch this business and share the value of its content once again. With this new re-edit, my speaker and training business has been put back on track, and a new, better Caveman has risen—wiser, more experienced, and more resilient than ever. This Caveman's shop is back open for business!

This book aimed to deliver a more straightforward way to manage daily struggles. Praise is the highest form of reward, and as an author, it is hard to know if this book has hit the mark. If you believe this book has enhanced your life, a great review on any of the author's platforms (Amazon or Goodreads) will make my day.

THE CAVEMAN PRINCIPLES

We only have one life; make it happy, one with less stress, and enjoy every day.

THE CAVEMAN PRINCIPLES